I LOVE ROCK 'N' ROLL
(Except When I Hate It)

I Love Rock 'n' Roll

(Except When I Hate It)

Extremely Important Stuff
About the Songs
and Bands You Love, Hate,
Love to Hate,
and Hate to Love

BRIAN BOONE

A Perigee Book

A PERIGEE BOOK
Published by the Penguin Group
Penguin Group (USA) Inc.
375 Hudson Street, New York, New York 10014, USA
Penguin Group (Canada), 90 Eglinton Avenue East, Suite 700, Toronto, Ontario M4P 2Y3, Canada (a division of Pearson Penguin Canada Inc.)
Penguin Books Ltd., 80 Strand, London WC2R 0RL, England
Penguin Group Ireland, 25 St. Stephen's Green, Dublin 2, Ireland (a division of Penguin Books Ltd.)
Penguin Group (Australia), 250 Camberwell Road, Camberwell, Victoria 3124, Australia (a division of Pearson Australia Group Pty. Ltd.)
Penguin Books India Pvt. Ltd., 11 Community Centre, Panchsheel Park, New Delhi—110 017, India
Penguin Group (NZ), 67 Apollo Drive, Rosedale, Auckland 0632, New Zealand (a division of Pearson New Zealand Ltd.)
Penguin Books (South Africa) (Pty.) Ltd., 24 Sturdee Avenue, Rosebank, Johannesburg 2196, South Africa

Penguin Books Ltd., Registered Offices: 80 Strand, London WC2R 0RL, England

While the author has made every effort to provide accurate telephone numbers and Internet addresses at the time of publication, neither the publisher nor the author assumes any responsibility for errors or for changes that occur after publication. Further, the publisher does not have any control over and does not assume any responsibility for author or third-party websites or their content.

Copyright © 2011 by Brian Boone
Text design by Kristin del Rosario

First edition: August 2011

Library of Congress Cataloging-in-Publication Data

Boone, Brian.
   I love rock 'n' roll (except when I hate it) : extremely important stuff about the songs and bands you love, hate, love to hate, and hate to love / Brian Boone.— 1st ed.
      p.   cm.
   ISBN 978-0-399-53679-3
   1. Rock music—Miscellanea. I. Title.
   ML3534.B662 2011
   781.66—dc22   2011010324

PRINTED IN THE UNITED STATES OF AMERICA

10 9 8 7 6 5 4 3 2 1

Most Perigee books are available at special quantity discounts for bulk purchases for sales promotions, premiums, fund-raising, or educational use. Special books, or book excerpts, can also be created to fit specific needs. For details, write: Special Markets, Penguin Group (USA) Inc., 375 Hudson Street, New York, New York 10014.

To Megan,
who is more captivating than any song,
and funnier than anything in this book.

«CONTENTS»

Music is kind of stupid.

I mean really. Why do I care so much about it? I have no musical talent; I've never been in a band. And yet, I can't stop buying music, listening to music, reading about music, or learning about how music is created. If I find a band I like, I want to memorize their entire collected output, then every member's misbegotten solo project, and then find out what led them to write that one particularly great song . . . and then find out what the hell was going wrong in their heads right before they made that one particularly shitty song.

But while music is a deeply cherished, very personal thing of which I am very passionate, I opt not to try and write a song, but instead will put on my headphones, or play *Rock Band* or watch *Glee*. Mainly this is because it's crazy hard to write a song, but it's also because finding emotional resonance in someone else's art connects me to the world. The Beach Boys' "God Only Knows" can still make me cry on the 10 billionth listen because it makes me acutely aware of the beauty and magic in the universe. However, when I hear the Beach Boys' "Kokomo" for the 10 billionth time, I feel hopelessly alienated from a world that would happily spend its money on a third-rate Jimmy Buffett knockoff.

Most everybody can agree that *Back to the Future*, *The Simpsons*, and *The Great Gatsby* are among the best of their respective worlds, but music is possibly the most polarizing of all media. For example, you know that I adore the Beach Boys in their period of Brian Wilson-led wild creativity in the mid-'60s, and hate them onward from when Mike Love took over to make "Kokomo" a sad reality. But perhaps you think that the Beach Boys grew unlistenable and weird when they stopped releasing three-minute songs about surfing, and that "Kokomo" is one of the greatest pop hits and comeback records of all time. While I appreciate you buying my book, and you are certainly entitled to your opinions, we can never be friends. Because you are just plain wrong about music, and probably everything else, too. See? *Polarizing*.

But here's the strange part: Bad music can be just as enjoyable as good music. What goes into the making of music is fascinating, sometimes more so than the actual bits of recorded noise. Knowing the details behind the music—and about how others responded to it—enhances my enjoyment of it. Or, it gives me more fodder to hate the stuff I hate. A good story is a good story.

Music, then, can be more than just sounds in a speaker in a moment. Good stories and interesting stuff about music makes an enjoyable, transcendent aural moment (good or bad) a full-on heart-, soul-, and mind-stimulating experience. Herein then, you will learn of: the time Disney tried to market Devo to kids; the ill-conceived first draft of "Thriller"; the pre-gangsta, smooth-lover Dr. Dre; how every band is related to the Pixies; which duet partners were sleeping with each other and which were just faking it; the Italian peasant inspiration for the metal "sign of the beast" gesture; and many more origins, meanings, stories, and interesting stuff.

CHAPTER 1

The Birth of (Mostly) Cool

ORIGINS AND BEGINNINGS

While the recording industry is essentially an apparatus to sell mildly appealing songs to fickle teenagers for a buck a pop, music fans consider it completely unacceptable when an authentic musician "sells out" with a sudden, cynical cash grab. (Bob Dylan making a Victoria's Secret ad, or quirky Nelly Furtado making booty-pop with Timbaland, for example.) But some artists have done it the other way around: They did the cheesy, commercial thing first, failed at it, and then found their niche and won the world over with artistic legitimacy. That would be

The Opposite of Selling Out

TRENT REZNOR'S OPTION 30

While '80s synth pop is just fine (I love New Order more than two of my three children), it's embarrassing and silly to admit that you like it when compared to, say, the dark, anguished, wrist-slashing mayhem of Nine Inch Nails. But when he was just starting out in professional

music in 1983, 18-year-old future NIN mastermind
Trent Reznor played keyboards and sang a bit in a poppy,
Human League-esque band called Option 30. The group
performed in dozens of Ohio and Pennsylvania clubs,
where its covers of Billy Idol, the Thompson Twins, and
Falco were crowd favorites. (Grasp the magnitude of that:
The guy who made "March of the Pigs" once covered
Falco.) In 1986, Reznor left the band, created Nine Inch
Nails, and just three years later released *Pretty Hate
Machine*. In other words, Reznor transformed into a tor-
mented, hollow, man-shaped vessel of self-loathing and
misanthropy because of one too many Thompson Twins
songs.

BILLY JOEL'S ATTILA

Off the top of my head, I would say that the thing that
I would want to hear the least in this world would
probably be, say, a psychedelic jazz/metal fusion band
fronted by Billy Joel. And that is actually a thing that
happened in real life. Joel played organ and keyboards
and his friend Jon Small played drums in the band
Attila. The duo released a self-titled album in 1970 (Joel
and Small are dressed as frightening ancient Mongolian
warriors—Huns—on the cover), which Joel referred
to in a 1985 interview as "psychedelic bullshit." The
exhaustive music encyclopedia *All Music Guide* goes a
bit further, declaring Attila's *Attila* to be "the worst
album released in the history of recorded music." And
although this sort of psychedelic bullshit was really
quite popular at the time (the Doors, Iron Butterfly, the
rest of your dad's record collection), the album tanked,

and Joel was so distraught, so convinced that his music career was over, that he tried to kill himself by drinking a bottle of furniture polish. Surprisingly, it's actually pretty tough to overdose on furniture polish, and the suicide didn't take, so Joel picked himself up and went on to marry a woman named Elizabeth Weber, who just so happened to be the ex-wife of Jon Small. For her, he wrote "Just the Way You Are" and "She's Always a Woman." Those are soft rock ballads, the kind of thing Joel was supposed to do with his life.

LENNY KRAVITZ *IS* ROMEO BLUE

In 1982, Kravitz graduated high school and successfully convinced his father, a jazz promoter, to let him use his college fund to pay for a demo—the boy wanted to become a musician. Specifically, he wanted to become the next Prince. With straightened and dyed blue hair, blue contact lenses, and blue makeup, Kravitz started calling himself "Romeo Blue." The music: similar but inferior to Prince, of course, specifically his late '70s overly sexualized funk-pop. Kravitz/Romeo Blue got some offers (including a deal with I.R.S. Records, which ultimately fell through), but was told by more than one industry big shot that his music wasn't black enough for black radio, and wasn't white enough for white radio (despite the fact that the act he ripped off, Prince, a black man, had his music played everywhere). Kravitz took a few years off, let the blue dye fade out of his hair, put in some dreadlocks, became a hippie, recorded the neo-funk/all-rock *Let Love Rule*, and released it in 1989 under his real name. He hasn't stopped rocking or attracting super-hot ladies since.

ALICE IN CHAINS WAS ALICE 'N CHAINZ

In 1985, Layne Staley formed the band Alice 'N Chainz. Despite the inclusion of a "z" in the name, this was not a rap-metal band, but one just barely on the legitimate side of hair metal. Alice 'N Chainz recorded a single demo in Seattle, and it sounded like the prevailing Seattle sound at the time: cheesy hard rock, a la Queensrÿche or Metal Church (grunge was not only not yet cool, it wasn't actually a thing that existed yet). The cover depicted Staley and his bandmates in big hair and tight pants, with this message in the liner notes: "if you are blonde, tan, tastey, and tight, the boyz in the band love you lots." Fortunately, in 1987, Staley met guitar virtuoso Jerry Cantrell and the two guys merged the boyz in their bands (Cantrell's band Diamond Lie was almost as ridiculous), and Alice in Chains, a glam-free, despair-heavy hard rock band (you know, grunge) was born.

DR. DRE'S WORLD CLASS WRECKIN' CRU

Nobody is harder than Dr. Dre, and never more than when he was in N.W.A., a band so badass that the first word of their name is a racial epithet so ugly and fearsome that all white people live in constant fear of accidentally saying it out loud. Dre defined rap in the '90s with his album *The Chronic*, which pioneered the era's pot-addled, thugs-with-guns-around-every-corner vibe. It's shocking then that Dr. Dre's first rap group was the World Class Wreckin' Cru. They were just a simple '80s pop rap group who did what rap groups thought was cool at the time: making wild hand gestures while they rapped, boasting about themselves and how good at the rapping they were, and wearing shiny outfits. Even Dre's sister (like, his actual, biological sister) Mona Lisa Young was in the group, mostly to sing hooks. By the time the group scored a minor hit with the bedroom-ready, Boyz II Men-ish romantic slow jam "Turn Off the Lights" in 1988, Dre, along with bandmate DJ Yella, had already left the World Class Wreckin' Cru to form the significantly harder N.W.A.

Titles are hard. Not only do they have to sum up a work and suggest a message about its content, but they also have to attractively market the whole damn thing. Titles are often decided way, way down the line in the creative process. Here's a look at some notable placeholders, these

Working Titles of Major Albums

PINK FLOYD, *Dark Side of the Moon* (1973)

At the end of 1971, Pink Floyd was preparing to tour a new song cycle called *Dark Side of the Moon: A Piece for Assorted Lunatics*. But just before hitting the road, the band learned that the up-and-coming British blues rock band Medicine Head was just weeks away from releasing an album that was titled, completely coincidentally, *Dark Side of the Moon*. So, Pink Floyd re-titled their project *Eclipse* after the name of one of the songs in the cycle. But then Medicine Head's *Dark Side of the Moon* failed to make much of an impression commercially, ostensibly reverting the title to fair-game status. In 1973, Pink Floyd released *The Dark Side of the Moon*, which, with a record 741 weeks on the *Billboard* album chart and 45 million copies sold, was slightly more successful than the Medicine Head album of the same name.

THE BEATLES, *The Beatles* (1968)

When the recording sessions for what is known as *The White Album* began (officially it's untitled, or self-titled), the band wanted to call it *A Doll's House*, after the late nineteenth-century proto-feminist play by Norwegian dramatist Henrik Ibsen. (Evidently, the Beatles were looking to break through to the only two demographics that had eluded them: college freshman theater majors and Norwegians who didn't like "Norwegian Wood.") The title wasn't meant to be. In July 1968, the British progressive rock band Family put out *Music in a Doll's House*. Unable to come up with any alternative album titles, and having simultaneously scrapped the planned cover of expressionist portraits of the Fab Four because it no longer seemed appropriate to illustrate a title-less project, the album was released in November 1968 with a plain white cover. The band never got around to picking a title, so the album didn't get one.

MICHAEL JACKSON, *Thriller* (1982)

Michael Jackson's *Thriller* could have been called *Starlight*, because the song "Thriller" was originally a song called "Starlight." A song with that title was certainly about a magical, periwinkle-colored unicorn named Starlight, right? Unfortunately, no. Producer Quincy Jones had hired keyboardist Rod Temperton of the band Heatwave ("Boogie Nights") to write songs for Michael Jackson's follow-up to *Off the Wall*, for which Temperton had written "Rock with You," an inexplicably successful combination of soft rock and funk. Using the same approach, Temperton wrote "Starlight," a track about a couple attempting to make a doomed relationship work. While Jones liked the song's ominous, repetitive, electronic bass loop, he didn't care for the lyrics, or the title, so he asked Temperton to come up with something else, something that could also serve as the album title. Temperton later told London's *Telegraph* that he wrote "two or three hundred titles" and settled on "Midnight Man." Then, the next morning, Temperton says, "Something in my head just said, this is the title. You could visualize it on top of the *Billboard* charts." That word: *Thriller*. Jones and Jackson also thought it was boss, so Temperton wrote new lyrics for "Starlight," mostly horror movie clichés, and that, in turn, became "Thriller."

THE OFFSPRING, *Splinter* (2003)

Mocking Axl Rose's then-10-year-long (and counting) quest to finish and release the near mythical Guns N' Roses album *Chinese Democracy*, the Offspring announced in 2003 that *its* next album would be called *Chinese Democracy*. Front man Dexter Holland told reporters it was done as an act of revenge—Rose had stolen his signature braided hair look for a surprise Guns N' Roses performance at the 2002 MTV Video Awards, so he was stealing Rose's famous, but technically unused, title. But none of the major media news outlets covering this story thought it was noteworthy to mention what day it was when Holland made his announcement: April 1, 2003. It was all an April Fool's Day joke/publicity stunt. Holland wasn't really angry that Rose had imitated his haircut, nor did he truly intend to name the Offspring's next album *Chinese Democracy*. When it came out the following winter, the album was titled *Splinter*, after a lyric in the song "Long Way Home." (The real GNR *Chinese Democracy*, by the way, would finally emerge five years later.)

NAS, *Untitled* (2008)

Nas, who usually has something interesting or provocative to express in his music, wanted to call his ninth album *Nigger*. Not surprisingly, this was a controversial choice. His label, Def Jam, fully supported him, but when Jesse Jackson and the NAACP publicly objected, Nas relented and released the album without an official title. The cover, however, still bore the very shocking image of Nas with slave-like whip scars on his back. So he made his point.

U2, *The Joshua Tree* (1987)

The U2 experience is pretty much an even split between soaring, angelic guitars and relentless pleading about social issues. As such, the Irish band nearly called the album that made them superstars in America *The Two Americas* because when they traveled in America, Bono and the others were shocked to realize that America was both highly romanticized and fraught with class divisions. (Because nobody has ever romanticized *Ireland* or dealt with overwhelming social divides in *Ireland*.) In the end, Bono decided that *The Joshua Tree* was a better title, because it more accurately reflected the album's recurring images of deserts, trees, and water.

BEASTIE BOYS, *Licensed to Ill* (1986)

Today, the Beastie Boys play electro-rap and are highly respected elder statesmen in, confusingly, the alternative rock community. But when they began in the 1980s, they were screechy frat boys making abrasive rap-metal. It was in those days that they nearly called their debut record the blustery, extraordinarily distasteful *Don't Be a Faggot*. Columbia Records, the corporate parent of the Beasties' label, Def Jam, flat-out refused to release an album called *Don't Be a Faggot* and made them change it to something else, anything else. In 1999, Beastie Adam Horovitz published an open letter in *Time Out New York* apologizing "to the entire gay and lesbian community for the shitty and ignorant things we said on our first record," as well as for the working title.

DAVIE BOWIE, *Low* (1977)

If Bowie had gone with his initial impulse, *Low* would have been titled *New Music Night and Day*, which sounds like the name of a Rudy Vallee revue from 1931. Bowie chose the optimistic title while trying to beat a cocaine addiction and while starting a new, more experimental chapter of his career with producer Brian Eno, who produced the album. All parties decided to call it *Low*, since most of the album was about fighting off the demons that come to the surface when you're recovering from a cocaine addiction.

ALICIA KEYS, *Songs in A Minor* (2001)

Keys was a protégé of important music executive Clive Davis, who signed her to his own label, J Records. Davis wouldn't let Keys call her debut *Soul Stories in A Minor* out of fear that only "soul" radio stations would play it. The title was changed to *Songs in A Minor*. The pun on Keys's (stage) name remained in play, and Keys indeed received heavy airplay, but only on radio stations that played "songs," so, like, all of them.

You probably pretend it's trite and stupid whenever you hear a drunk or a hipster or a drunk hipster shout out "Free Bird!" at a concert. But you secretly think it's hilarious, and you also think a sea of aloft lighters is breathtaking. Actually, those

Concert Clichés

are why you keep going to concerts at all.

SHOUTING "'FREE BIRD!'"

In 1976, Lynyrd Skynyrd was recording their live album *One More from the Road* at the Fabulous Fox Theatre in Atlanta. Throughout their set and the first encore, they still hadn't played their best and most popular song, the 1973 epic "Free Bird." The crowd, having to sit through a couple of hours of Lynyrd Skynyrd songs that were not "Free Bird," grew agitated and started to chant, "'Free Bird!' 'Free Bird!'" As captured on the album, singer Ronnie Van Zandt asked the audience, "What song is it you wanna hear?" to which the audience responded, "'Free Bird!'" At that point, the band finally played it.

But this is only an indirect ancestor of the phenomenon. In 1988, Chicago radio personality Kevin Matthews learned that Florence Henderson—the sometime singer and one-time *Brady Bunch* star—was coming to town for a concert. Matthews thought it would be fun to liven up the show and torment Henderson if a bunch of people went to the show and relentlessly shouted requests to play "Free Bird." It became a Chicago tradition to shout it at other lame concerts, and soon, all concerts.

But that might not be the true origin, either. *Chicago Tribune* music writer Greg Kot told a *Wall Street Journal* reporter investigating the "Free Bird" phenomenon that he remembers it being shouted at alternative rock shows in the early '80s, ostensibly as a way for indie rock snots to let their disdain for mainstream rock be known, even though simply being at an indie rock show is probably enough to establish indie cred.

It's now shouted at every single concert every single day, and musicians respond to it in different ways. Chris Kirkwood of the Meat Puppets (among others) says "I've got your 'free bird' right here," and then flips the bird; Phish sings a section of it a capella; and the Dandy Warhols sometimes actually go ahead and play the song in its entirety in a pithy meta-joke played on the jokester. (Florence Henderson, for the record, has still never performed "Free Bird" in part or in its entirety.)

LIGHTERS

The first night of the 1969 Woodstock festival was hammered by a nasty thunderstorm, perhaps God's way of punishing the half million assembled dirty hippies and their terrible, terrible music. It was almost totally dark and the rain was pouring down as folk singer Melanie prepared to take the stage, so organizers passed out candles to the crowd. Before the audience of 500,000 attempted to smoke, snort, or inject the candles, the stage announcer instructed the audience to "light a candle to keep away the rain" in a well meaning but woefully naive understanding of meteorology. Melanie sheepishly took the stage and began to perform; as she did, the candles began to spark alive and Melanie comfortably performed to a receptive crowd, even though most were soaking wet, freezing cold, and really, really high.

Melanie was so moved by the experience, particularly the sight of a sea of longhairs holding tiny bits of light, that she wrote a song about it called "Lay Down (Candles in the Rain)." It was released in 1970 and became her first hit, reaching #6 on the *Billboard* Hot 100. It became a tradition at Melanie concerts throughout the '70s to light candles during performances of the song in an effort to re-create the night at Woodstock. The concept spread to other concerts, and candles were replaced by something more common in the concertgoer's pocket: cigarette lighters, back when you could smoke inside of North America. Fans now hold up their display-lit cell phones. In 2010, the BIC lighter company introduced a smartphone app that fills the device's screen with a photo of a lit lighter. The effect of thousands of those held up is not so much breathtaking as much as it is uncomfortably reminiscent of the cell-phone chatter-control room from *The Dark Knight*.

LIGHT SHOWS

Without seemingly random, acid-trip-inspired images projected on a cyclorama behind the band, how would you even know that you were at a rock concert? In 1966, the Byrds tossed a series of randomly flashing colored lights onto a white backdrop at a show at the Village Gate in New York City. Bill Graham, the legendary promoter and controller of the Fillmore Auditorium in San Francisco, thought the Byrds were onto something, and he began to stage random light shows for the psychedelic bands playing at his club. The idea was an immediate smash in San Francisco, where other designers incorporated the trippy imagery to complement the insane lyrics of Jefferson Airplane and whatever drugs the audience were enjoying that evening. But simultaneously, and completely independently of the Byrds and Graham shows, other light artists were beginning to stage their works to accompany bands in Southern California, London, and elsewhere. By 1970, swirling lasers were an integral part of most big rock shows in the United States and Great Britain.

So who was the first mighty metal god to throw the devil horns hand sign? Like metal itself, the story is sludgy, murky, and slightly incoherent. But praise be to the metal gods, whichever one it may be, for giving us a way to express ourselves

When a Song Rocks So Hard That All You Can Do Is Form Your Hand Into a Menacing, Demonic Gesture

COVEN INVENTED IT . . .

Formed in 1967 by Jinx Dawson (a lady), Coven was a proto-metal band that blatantly promoted Satanism (as opposed to latter-day metal bands, which merely imply Satanism). Dawson began and ended all Coven concerts by making the devil horns, suggesting that it was a "hoo-ray for Satan" kind of thing. It became Coven's trademark, and the band members threw the sign on the back cover photograph of its marvelously titled first album *Witchcraft Destroys Minds & Reaps Souls* (1969), which ends with a recording of a real Satanic mass.

. . . BUT RONNIE JAMES DIO POPULARIZED IT

The concept of the "evil eye" occurs throughout many ancient cultures. In short, it's the idea that a spirit will lay a devastating curse onto the envious. In Italy, it dates back to ancient Rome, where a certain gesture was made to ward off the evil eye—the pinky and index finger extended, while the middle and ring fingers formed a fist with the thumb. It was meant to depict the penis going into the vagina, as the sexual imagery was said to distract and repel the evil eye. (Curses, evil, penetration: It's all *extremely* metal.) The gesture also looked like horns, and so in Italy and other Mediterranean cultures, the sign came to be known as the *corna*, which is Italian for "horns."

Ronnie James Dio joined Black Sabbath in 1979, replacing original singer Ozzy Osbourne. Osbourne often made the two-fingered "peace" gesture to the audience, and Dio wanted to continue the tradition, but with some gesture of his own. So he did something he remembered his Italian grandmother would do to fend off the evil eye, which she called Moloch: She'd hold her two outer fingers out, with the inner fingers balled up with the thumb. As Black Sabbath was the most popular and influential of all metal bands, fans (and other bands) appropriated Dio's horn-like gesture and it spread.

OR MAYBE BLACKIE LAWLESS POPULARIZED IT . . .

Prior to fronting W.A.S.P., Blackie Lawless was in a '70s metal band called Sister. While reading a book about the occult one night (as all metal gods do in their spare time), he learned about an ancient Italian custom of using a gesture used to ward off the evil eye called the *corna*. Lawless thought it was pretty badass, so he started using it in performances in 1977, a couple of years before Ronnie James Dio started doing the same thing.

. . . AND THEN GENE SIMMONS STOLE IT

In 1977, three months after Gene Simmons saw Sister perform in Los Angeles, his band KISS released *Love Gun*. On the cover, Simmons makes the corna. He has denied lifting it from Lawless (or Coven, or Dio), claiming he came up with it on his own, albeit inadvertently. He holds his bass pick in his middle two fingers, and so when he raises his arm aloft in metal triumph, his pick still clutched tightly, he can't help but make the gesture, which, intentional or not, still technically pledges his allegiance to the Dark Lord . . . Clive Davis.

<< ▭ >>

"Super" is quite often a prelude to major disappointment, as in *Superman Returns*, or with

wherein a bunch of massive talents—or massive egos—get together to make a whole that is usually way less than the sum of its parts.

THE DIRTY MAC

In 1968, the Rolling Stones taped a special for British television called *The Rolling Stones Rock and Roll Circus*, in which they and other bands played on a set decorated like a circus. One of those acts was a one-off supergroup called the Dirty Mac. Put together by John Lennon, the band also featured Keith Richards of the Rolling Stones, drummer Mitch Mitchell of the Jimi Hendrix Experience, and Eric Clapton, at the time a part of Cream, which itself was a supergroup. Such an assemblage should have been a definitive rock 'n' roll moment, but the Dirty Mac's set paled to that of the Who, who delivered such an electrifying performance that they overshadowed all of the other acts. That's reportedly why the Rolling Stones wouldn't allow the show to be seen until 1996, nearly three decades later, when it came out on home video.

DAMN YANKEES

Between 1990 and 1992, at the tail end of the hair metal/arena rock era of popular music, Damn Yankees released two albums, as well as the quintessential monster ballad "High Enough." Damn Yankees consisted of crossbow hunter and occasional guitarist Ted Nugent, Tommy Shaw of Styx, Jack Blades of Night Ranger, and Michael Cartellone, a drummer Shaw met when he was working in the art department of a New York children's clothing store. Cartellone then continued to earn supergroup credentials, as he's now the drummer for Lynyrd Skynyrd.

MAD SEASON

Considering the high volume of rock stars with substance abuse problems, it's surprising that more bands don't originate in rehab facilities. In 1994, Pearl Jam guitarist Mike McCready checked into recovery in Minneapolis and met John Baker Saunders, a bassist who had played in a bunch of blues bands. They became

friends, and upon their release from the tank they went
to Seattle to jam with McCready's good friend, Alice in
Chains vocalist Layne Staley, and drummer Barrett Martin of the lesser-known Seattle band Screaming Trees.
With contributions from members of three of the biggest bands of the era, Mad Season only managed a single
rock radio hit, "River of Deceit."

THE HIGHWAYMEN

The originators of the '70s "outlaw country" subgenre
(well-written story songs by rough-and-tumble, slightly
boozy badasses) had worked with each other here and
there, but not until 1985 did Johnny Cash, Waylon Jen-
nings, Willie Nelson, and Kris Kristofferson all record
together. The album *Highwayman* sold a million copies
and hit #1 on the country album chart, leading to a second release, *Highwayman 2*, in 1990, on which the group
used the name the Highwaymen for the first time. It was
this project that began Cash's remarkable (solo) comeback that lasted until his death in 2003.

TRAVELING WILBURYS

In 1988, George Harrison was in Los Angeles and needed
to record a B-side for a single, so he approached the producer he'd just used for his album *Cloud Nine*, Jeff Lynne
of the Electric Light Orchestra. Lynne was busy working
on a Roy Orbison album and said yes to Harrison, who
also asked Orbison to participate, because, hey, it was
Roy Orbison and he was just there, hanging out. Before
he could record the single though, Harrison had to make

another L.A. big-shot pit stop at the home of Tom Petty, so as to retrieve one of his favorite guitars, which Petty had been borrowing. Petty let him have the guitar back, on one condition: that he could be part of what was becoming a pretty stellar B-side recording session. A few days later, Harrison, Lynne, Orbison, and Petty booked a studio, which happened to be a private home studio, in the home of Bob Dylan. Meeting to just record a song, the new friends (Dylan was part of the thing now, too) ended up recording a whole album as the Traveling Wilburys. *Traveling Wilburys Vol. 1*, propelled by the staggering novelty of the idea of five superstars synchronizing their schedules, sold three million copies in the United States in 1988, leading to a quick regrouping to record a follow-up. Before that could happen, however, Orbison died. The rest of the band lobbied '60s pop singer Del Shannon to fill the slot . . . but then he died, too. The sort-of humorously titled *Traveling Wilburys Vol. 3* (because it was their *second* album) was released by the suddenly four-piece Wilburys and sold about a third as many copies as the first one did. The Wilburys then traveled in different directions.

BLIND FAITH

In 1968, Eric Clapton's group Cream broke up. At about the same time, Steve Winwood's Traffic broke up, too. Clapton and Winwood had wanted to work together for years, and now they finally had some time to get together for some jam sessions. The gatherings were rounded out by bassist Ric Grech (a friend and jam session partner, separately, of both Clapton and Winwood), and another ex-bandmate on drums: Ginger Baker of Cream. The resulting supergroup became a one-stop shop for tedious British blues-rock. Their only album, the self-titled *Blind Faith*, went to #1 in the United States.

ASIA

Though the one-word name made it sound like just another early-'80s arena rock band (Journey, Survivor, Foreigner), Asia's members were firmly entrenched in the far-out, pretentious, keyboard riffing jackassery of progressive rock. (The airbrushed prisms and space imagery on Asia's album covers would be a clear clue—or warning—to this fact.) In 1981, former King Crimson bassist John Wetton and Yes guitarist Steve Howe were hired by Geffen Records to write and produce songs. They started to play with drummer Carl Palmer (of Emerson, Lake, and Palmer). When it became clear that they needed a keyboardist, Palmer called up his old bandmate Geoff Downes, with whom he had briefly been in Yes in the early '80s (following Downes's time in the Buggles). Asia's 1982 self-titled album spawned the #4 hit "Heat of the Moment," which is the only catchy, accessible song on an album full of long-winded, unmelodic keyboard instrumentation. (You know, *prog rock*.) Still, it sold four million copies.

THEM CROOKED VULTURES

Most supergroups represent the cream, or at least icons, of one particular era, genre, or scene of music. Them Crooked Vultures, formed in 2009, spans generations:

The bassist is John Paul Jones of Led Zeppelin; Dave Grohl of Nirvana and Foo Fighters plays drums; Josh Homme of Queens of the Stone is the lead guitarist and vocalist; and the rhythm guitarist is Alain Johannes, best known for being in the '80s California band What Is This?, of which three other members left to become part of the Red Hot Chili Peppers. Despite a high profile launch, including an appearance on *Saturday Night Live*, a top 10 alternative rock hit in "New Fang," and a promise to get back into the studio to record a second album to meet perceived demand, the album *Them Crooked Vultures* sold modestly, around 300,000 copies, or, viewed another way, a hell of a lot less than the recent releases by both the Foo Fighters and Queens of the Stone Age.

Back in the olden days, say you wanted to form a musical combo (either an a capella group or a string quartet— there were no other options in the olden days), and say your name was Jeffrey Marvin. Your group would therefore be named the Jeffrey Marvin Combo. But then rock came along, allowing us to leave such stuffy and pretentious names behind. Today, bands can give themselves wholesome, straightforward names, like Death Cab for Cutie or Arcade Fire. Here is a look into

How Bands Got Their Stupid Names

Remember in high school when you had to form a pretend business for a class, and you couldn't think of anything for a name, so you just put together the first initials of everyone in the group to form an acronym? That's how Doug, Brendan, and I formed BDB Coal Inc. during a unit on the Industrial Age, and it's also how the endlessly popular Swedish pop band **ABBA** named itself. The letters stand for Agnetha (Fältskog), Benny (Andersson), Björn (Ulvaeus), and Anni-Frid (Lyndstad).

In the late 1960s, Australian teenager Margaret Young saw the letters **AC/DC** on a sewing machine and suggested it as a possible band name to her musician brothers, Angus and Malcolm Young, who thought it was a good name, since it meant something to do with power . . . raw, *metal* power.

Guitarist Win Butler told *Rolling Stone* in 2005 about how somebody once told him about a fire that destroyed a New Hampshire arcade in the early '80s, which claimed the lives of several teenagers. The story turned out to be an urban legend, but Butler thought the spooky, mysterious name **ARCADE FIRE** fit his spooky, mysterious band perfectly.

Since they all wore plaid Pendleton shirts, an early 1960s California pop band called itself the Pendletones. But when they received their first pressing of singles from Candix Records in 1961, the company had labeled them the work of the **BEACH BOYS** to associate the group with the emerging surf rock sound. The name stuck.

The **BEE GEES** could and should stand for "Brothers Gibb," but it doesn't, really. The band started off with that name in the '50s, and an Australian DJ named Bill Gates started playing their songs, which led to some high-profile club dates that were booked by a promoter named Bill Goode. And so, they changed the name of the group to the Bee Gees, Goode's and Gates's initials, as a subtle tribute.

Did you ever watch that weird European cartoon on Nickelodeon in the '80s about the little boy and his gigantic white dog that were always on the lam in pastoral France for some reason? That was *Belle and Sebastian*. That's where the Scottish pop group **BELLE AND SEBASTIAN** got the name.

Mississippi-born bassist Brad Smith's dad was fond of calling hippies "blind melons," an obscure and impenetrable Southern slang term meaning "unemployed hippies." And as Brad Smith and his friends were also a bunch of unemployed hippies, they named their band **BLIND MELON**.

Richard and Karen Carpenter named their duo after themselves, but they named it **CARPENTERS**, not *the* Carpenters, because, as Richard Carpenter wrote in the liner notes for a Carpenters greatest hits compilation, they thought that not having that definite article made them sound "hipper," à la "Buffalo Springfield or Jefferson Airplane." It didn't really work.

Members of the thumping, booty-shaking, dance-rock band **!!!** (pronounced "chik-chik-chik") got the idea from *The Gods Must Be Crazy*, the '80s movie series about

African Bushmen in which the tongue clicks of the natives' languages were represented as "!" in the English subtitles.

While attending University College London in 1996, Chris Martin formed a band with some friends. They first performed under the names Pectoralz and Starfish, but ultimately decided to ask another student musician, Tim Crompton, if they could use the name of his defunct band for their active band: **COLDPLAY**. Crompton obliged. He, in turn, had taken the name from obscure American poet Phillip Horky's collection *Child's Reflection, Cold Play*.

There's an old English nursery rhyme about counting crows to tell your fortune: "One for sorrow, two for joy, three for girls, four for boys, five for silver, six for gold, seven for a secret never to be told." Singer Adam Duritz loved the poem as a child, and lifted **COUNTING CROWS** for a band name.

There once was an Irish modern rock band called Cranberries Saw Us, a pun of "cranberry sauce." When Dolores O'Riordan joined the band, she asked the band to shorten it to just the **CRANBERRIES**, and they did, because "Cranberries Saw Us" is silly.

After their label head dismissed their initial band name idea in 1967, this band now no longer named the Golliwogs toyed around with a series of other silly names, including Deep Bottle Blue, Muddy Rabbit, and Credence Nuball and the Ruby. According to Hank Bordowitz in

Bad Moon Rising, guitarist Tom Fogerty rattled them all off to a friend one day, who told him that, amazingly, he had a coworker whose name really was Credence Nuball. (He came to meet the band at a San Francisco show.) Adding an extra "e," to create "creedence" (as in something to believe in), the band took that and added to it an inspiration from a magazine ad for Clearwater beer, made with "cool, clear water." Fogerty, thinking the name needed a third word, settled on "revival," as in a religious revival show, because it sounded good after the other two words. Boom: **CREEDENCE CLEARWATER REVIVAL**.

After leading the band Further Seems Forever, Chris Carrabba went solo. In the song "The Sharp Hint of New Tears," there's a lyric about confessing secrets aloud to nobody but your car. Carrabba altered that into the name for his new project, **DASHBOARD CONFESSIONAL**.

While **DEAD KENNEDYS** may sound like a purposely offensive, punk rock attempt at blunt shock value, thoughtful front man Jello Biafra attests that the name is a metaphor for the death of the American Dream.

The Bonzo Dog Doo-Dah Band, a jokey rock group (member Neil Innes was later part of the Rutles with Eric Idle), performed a song called "**DEATH CAB FOR CUTIE**" in the Beatles movie *Magical Mystery Tour*. When Seattle-area guitarist and Beatles fan Ben Gibbard of the indie band Pinwheel started recording modest solo works in 1992, he took on the name and carried it over when he formed a full band five years later.

Many Communist and anti-Communist uprisings throughout the last 200 years have been remembered for and named after the months in which they occurred, which makes them sound dramatic, and also makes you realize that they didn't last long and weren't successful. The Decembrist Revolt happened in imperialist Russia in December 1825, in which 3,000 troops (called "Decembrists") marched in protest of the ascension to power of a bourgeois czar, which historians say helped lay the foundation for the adoption of Communism a century later. When he formed his band in Portland in 2001, Colin Meloy anglicized "Decembrists" to the **DECEMBERISTS**. True to its namesake, the band occasionally opens shows with the old Soviet national anthem, which is the kind of thing you'd expect from a Portland indie rock band.

A "doobie" is what dudes in their late thirties with mustaches thought hip people called marijuana in the '70s. The **DOOBIE BROTHERS** were dudes in their late thirties that had mustaches in the '70s.

DURAN DURAN played many of its early gigs at the Barberella, a nightclub in Birmingham, England, so it named itself after Dr. Durand-Durand, the villain in the Jane Fonda '60s camp classic *Barbarella*.

When a band gives those who ask multiple stories about how it found a name, chances are all of them are false and the name is ultimately meaningless. So it is with the **FLAMING LIPS**. Founder Wayne Coyne has variously said it's a drug reference, the name of a '70s porno movie, or that he had a dream in which the Virgin Mary kissed him while she was on fire.

World War II fighter pilots called UFOs **FOO FIGHTERS**. Dave Grohl picked that as the name for his post-Nirvana band because he had a longtime fascination with UFOs, which is fitting. When Grohl was shopping around demos of the band's first album (recorded almost completely by Grohl alone), he wanted it to get attention for its musical merits, not because it was made by the guy from Nirvana, so he didn't put any identifying material on it (besides contact info). In other words, Foo Fighters was "unidentified."

When hastily throwing together a collaboration, rapper Cee-Lo and DJ Danger Mouse couldn't think of a name, so they swiped **GNARLS BARKLEY** from the name of a mutual friend's fantasy basketball team. (You know what else would have been good? Snarl Malone. Or maybe Tragic Johnson. Scary Bird?)

When L.A. Guns and Hollywood Rose merged in 1985, and after the merger was approved by the Federal Hair Band Trade Commission, the bands' names were merged, too, to form **GUNS N' ROSES**.

Surprisingly, **HOLE** is not a characteristically blunt sexual reference from the mind of Courtney Love. Instead, Love said her mother used to tell her that she "can't walk around with a big hole inside yourself," according to a 1990 interview with *Flipside*. But it's also a reference to a favorite quotation of Love's from the Greek tragedy *Medea*: "There's a hole that pierces my soul."

A moody British band called Warsaw formed in 1976, but there was another band making the London club rounds at the time called Warsaw Pakt, so to avoid confusion, Warsaw changed its name to **JOY DIVISION**, the name for the prostitution sectors of Nazi concentration camps where prisoners were used as sexual slaves for Nazi officers. Fun name! The band all made a pact that should anyone ever leave the band for any reason, the name "Joy Division" would no longer be used. Well, singer Ian Curtis left the band in 1980 by way of suicide. The rest opted to continue, and needing a new name, liked the suggestion **NEW ORDER**, offered up by their manager Rob Gretton, who'd spotted the words in a newspaper article titled "The People's New Order of Kampuchea." And while Adolf Hitler called his sadistic drive toward world domination "the new order of the Third Reich" in *Mein Kampf*, it's purely coincidental that the same group of people chose, again, a name with Nazi connotations.

In the 2001 video for New Order's "Crystal," a fictional band called the **KILLERS** plays in a club scene. When Las Vegas musician Brandon Flowers (whose favorite band is New Order) formed a band, he used the name, which, as of press time, contains no specific, outright, or obscure allusions to Nazism.

KINGS OF LEON is a family band—three brothers and a cousin—and their shared grandfather's name is Leon, and they are his spawn, or in pet-name parlance, his kings. It also works as a pun, as Léon is a region that's now part of France, but which was an independent monarchy, or kingdom, from the tenth to the fourteenth centuries.

At the peak of their fire-breathing, blood-spitting evil Kabuki heyday, **KISS** were forced to explain to reporters that they were not really devil-worshipping Satanists, a rumor spread by parents' groups who said the band's name was an acronym for "knights in Satan's service." Lead singer Paul Stanley attested that he chose KISS because he was looking for something that sounded simultaneously sexy and dangerous, the mood he was trying to convey with the band's songs.

Rumored to be an acronym for "Kill Motherfucking Depeche Mode," **KMFDM** actually stands for *"kein mehr-heit fur die mitleid,"* a German phrase that translates as "no majority for the pity," an act of intentional grammatical incorrectness by group leader Sascha Konietzko, who reportedly got the words for the name together by randomly assembling headlines cut out of German newspapers.

Former (and, by now, current) tattoo artist Fred Durst once had a dog named Biscuit who limped. He changed the spelling to have a *Z* and a *K* instead of an *S* and a *C*, because that's just what rap metal bands do, and thus he created **LIMP BIZKIT**.

MY BLOODY VALENTINE picked its name from a 1981 slasher film of the same name, which is a play on the old standard "My Funny Valentine." *My Bloody Valentine* was remade in 2009, so in 2027 some new band will likely come along and remake every My Bloody Valentine song.

MODEST MOUSE was taken from a line in Virginia Woolf's short story "The Mark on the Wall," in which the middle-class are described as "modest, mouse-coloured people."

MY MORNING JACKET is a "backronym," or a series of words cobbled together from an acronym. Lead singer Jim James says he saw the letters MMJ on an old jacket, and came up with the words to describe both the jacket and to name his band.

Trent Reznor told a zine in 1994 that he made a list of potential band names and settled on **NINE INCH NAILS** because it still sounded good after two weeks and it "could be easily abbreviated."

PEARL JAM has been evasive about its name origins, telling magazines or spreading rumors that (1) Eddie Vedder's cool grandma Pearl made a peyote jelly, that is, "Pearl's Jam; (2) it sounded like a cool combination of a P-word and J-word, having been inspired by the initials of legendary NBA coach Phil Jackson; (3) it was supposedly the nickname of pro baseball player Mookie Blaylock, with Mookie Blaylock having been the band's original, rejected name; or (4) it means semen, and the band thought it would be funny if the fans they figured they'd eventually attract, misogynistic frat boys, would proudly and unknowingly wear T-shirts emblazoned with a slang term for spooge.

PHISH's drummer is named John Fishman, and Phish is a calculated misspelling of the Fish in Fishman, the band's way of paying a small tribute to the Beatles (whose name is a play on "beetles").

Filipino guitarist Joey Santiago was learning English and noticed the word "pixie" in a book. His American bandmates thought it would be funny to have a big, burly guy like their singer Frank Black front a band called the **PIXIES**.

When asked how he came up with the name **QUEEN**, Freddie Mercury—and remember that this is in the '70s, when it didn't even occur to most people that Mercury might not be the rough-and-tumble man's man in exactly the way that they thought—said that he liked it because it was "strong," "universal," "immediate," and conjured up a lot of imagery, such as the glamorous and regal image of royalty.

Former child actor (*Salute Your Shorts*) and musician Blake Sennett says he had a dream in which he was being chased by a sports almanac. When he caught it, he flipped through it and came across an entry about an Australian-rules football player named **RILO KILEY**.

Before music, Malcolm McLaren ran a hip London clothing shop called Sex. When he assembled a punk band, it was to promote Sex (the store, not the thing married people do). So he called the group the **SEX PISTOLS**, which is pretty much just a euphemism for dicks, and was thus way punk rock.

Icelandic singer Jón Þór Birgisson has a younger sister named Sigurrós, who was born the same day he formed a band in 1994. It's quite a coincidence, then, that that band went on to be called **SIGUR RÓS**.

SONIC YOUTH achieved prominence after its members were well into their 30s, so the name is now a bit ironic. Thurston Moore came up with it in 1981—the Sonic is a tribute to Fred "Sonic" Smith of the pioneering proto-punk band the MC5, and the Youth alluded to the then-current fad of reggae bands using the word in their names (Big Youth and Musical Youth, for example).

In 1991, San Diego grunge band Mighty Joe Young was all set to record its first album when their producer told them they couldn't legally use their name, as it belonged to an old blues musician. Singer Scott Weiland had a backup plan: He thought STP motor oil stickers were cool, and so he worked backward to come up with a name to fit the acronym (a "backronym," like from before!). The band decided on **STONE TEMPLE PILOTS** after reject-ing other random assemblages of S-, T- and P-words, including Stereo Temple Pirates and, most regrettably, Shirley Temple's Pussy.

Styx is the river of death in the mythological Greek underworld of Hades, and while I'd assume it's where the members of the band **STYX** met in 1970, singer

Dennis DeYoung told *Circus* magazine in 1979 that out of "hundreds" of names bandied about, "Styx" was the only one "that none of us hated."

The favorite band of college media studies professors, and only college media studies professors, **TALKING HEADS** named themselves after a cynical slang term that takes a jab at the hollowness of television. A "talking head" is a TV news camera shot showing only a pundit's head and shoulders. Even though this seems like the kind of thing the band members would have learned at the place they formed, art school, it was actually lifted from an article in the very un-art-schooly periodical *TV Guide*.

Jane Fairchild, the girlfriend of singer Danny Hutton, suggested **THREE DOG NIGHT** for a band name, having read a magazine article about the Australian Aboriginal custom of snuggling up with dogs (or even dingos, if you weren't a delicious baby) to keep warm at night. A "one dog night," Fairchild learned, was relatively warm, while a "three dog night" was technically the coldest.

According to an interview Dean and Gene Ween (stage names) did on, improbably, NPR's *All Things Considered*, **WEEN** is a combination of *wuss*, which is an abbreviation of *wussy*, itself a slang contraction of *wimp* and *pussy*; and *peen*, which is short for *penis*. Bear in mind that Ween formed when its principal members were 15 years old.

While it's true that former Deep Purple singer David Coverdale once owned an albino python—that is, a white snake—inspiring the name of his later band **WHITESNAKE**, you just *know* that he was probably referring to his *other* white snake.

Front man Billy Gibbons wrote in his memoir *Rock + Roll Gearhead* that **ZZ TOP** was originally named ZZ King in tribute to blues legend B.B. King. Realizing that that sounded almost identical to B.B. King, the band went with "top" because that's what B.B. King was to them. Here's another fun ZZ Top fact: Whenever you publish an alphabetically arranged list about music, you are required by law to end it with something about ZZ Top.

CHAPTER 2

About a Song

UNFAMILIAR STORIES OF FAMILIAR TUNES

You know that song you like, and how you think you know what it means?

That Song, I Do Not Think It Means What You Think It Means

IT'S ABOUT HOW AMERICA SUCKS, NOT ABOUT HOW AMERICA IS AWESOME

In 1984, the Ronald Reagan reelection campaign co-opted Bruce Springsteen's "Born in the U.S.A." for use at rallies. They stopped when Springsteen sent a cease-and-desist letter, and frankly, the campaign should have thanked him for saving them from the continued embarrassment. Having only evidently read the title of the song, campaign officials were not aware that the song is a first-person account of a Vietnam War veteran who returns to the United States, can't get work, and ultimately lands in prison. In other words, "Born in the U.S.A." is a bitter, four-minute indictment of nearly every policy of the Regan administration.

IT'S ABOUT ORGASMS, NOT DYING

Cutting Crew's "(I Just) Died in Your Arms" is not a melodramatic, overwrought '80s love song about an affair so passionate, the narrator could, like, *gasp*, totally *die* in your arms (tonight). It's actually a sneakily dirty, filthy, shameful song. As reported in *The Billboard Book of Number One Hits*, the phrase "I just died in your arms" popped into Cutting Crew lead singer Nick Van Eede's head one night while he was popping his girlfriend. That phrase is the English version of *le petite mort*, or "the little death," a French slang euphemism for "orgasm." (Also, if you "die" all over your partner's arms, you're either doing it very, very wrong, or very, very right.)

IT'S ABOUT HEROIN, NOT A GIRL

"There She Goes" by the La's failed to make much of an impression when it was first released in 1988, but in 1990 it became a minor hit upon re-release. It ultimately became an all-time pop classic because of its bouncy hook and playful lyrics, presumably about a pretty girl the singer is crushing on, so much so that she's even coursing through his veins. Our narrator is in love, but the "she" is most likely sweet lady H (heroin, not Preparation). In M. W. Macefield's 2003 book *In Search of the La's*, La's guitarist Paul Hemmings flat-out dismissed the idea that "There She Goes" was about anything other than an adorable hipster girl, while the song's writer, La's singer Lee Mavers, has never explicitly said if it is or if it is not about drugs, but then his word isn't all that reliable, as he's been rumored to have an on-again, off-again relationship with, uh, heroin.

Presumably, when the song was covered in 1999 by crossover Christian pop band Sixpence None the Richer, the group had no idea it was about horse. And it's certain that nobody at Ortho-McNeil Pharmaceutical knew the song's real meaning when the company licensed the Sixpence version for use in a commercial for Ortho Tri-Cyclen, a birth control pill. So when you think of Christian bands unwittingly endorsing birth control pills, laugh harder, because they're also unwittingly endorsing heroin.

IT'S ABOUT FAT WOMEN, NOT STRONG WOMEN

In 2008, Hallmark introduced a line of greeting cards with sound chips inside that played familiar songs when opened. One card, for example, had written out on the front "a long time ago in a galaxy far, far away . . . you were born" and then the *Star Wars* theme plays. *Wocka-wocka*. A Mother's Day card, meanwhile, intended to go to a person's wife, was embedded with the Commodores' funk classic "Brick House." Hallmark had overlooked the fact that calling a woman a "brick house" is not a reference to her moral strength, nor is it a lustful admiration of her womanly figure. No, "she's a brick house" was a '70s slang term that basically meant "thoroughly and sizably built," that is, fat. And this was supposed to go to a person's wife, on Mother's Day.

IT'S ABOUT CAMUS, NOT ARABS

Robert Smith confirmed in a fan club newsletter in 1991 that the Cure's "Killing an Arab" is based on the major plot point of Albert Camus's 1942 novel *The Stranger*, in which the emotionally hollow, terribly existential narrator kills an Algerian man on a beach. If you didn't know that, this song could seem extremely racist and bluntly violent, what with its subject matter regarding the killing of Arabs.

IT'S ABOUT NUCLEAR ANNIHILATION, NOT POTENTIAL

Like "Born in the U.S.A.," grasping the meaning of Timbuk 3's 1986 hit "The Future's So Bright, I Gotta Wear Shades" is as simple as paying attention past the title of the song and listening to the lyrics. The song tells a story of a dim-witted, shortsighted nuclear scientist who gets X-ray vision from prolonged exposure to radiation. So it's not that the future is so promising, so incredibly momentous that it is metaphorically bright, it's that the future itself is literally, physically bright due to the blinding flash of all the nuclear bombs that will be dropped in the inevitable world-ending atomic Armageddon with the Soviets. (The shades won't help you. Duck and cover instead.) This knowledge will now make you feel uncomfortable every time you watch one of the many '80s movie comedies about upward mobility in which this song appears. You're welcome.

IT'S ABOUT HOW WOMEN ARE MEAN, NOT AN INVITATION TO GET HIGH

Yes, yes, yes, in Bob Dylan's "Rainy Day Women #12 & 35," he says, "everybody must get stoned." Woo! Pot!

Whatever. Dylan is characteristically and unsurprisingly less than forthcoming about the exact meaning of his lyrics (or he's stated them bluntly and nobody could understand what the hell he'd said), but several critics theorize that the song is about the Shirley Jackson style of getting stoned, wherein stoning is a metaphor for the song's "never can please them bitches" take on relationships. In other words, fellas, you're damned if you do, and damned if you don't. This song, while released in 1966, is basically a standup comedy routine from 1988 about the maddening but amusing differences between men and women

IT'S ABOUT HOW LOVE IS STUPID, NOT ABOUT HOW LOVE IS GREAT

Don't believe the title or your sensitive college boyfriend: R.E.M.'s "The One I Love" is not a love song. Michael Stipe meant for it to be stone-faced sarcastic. Earnest lovers generally don't call their beloved a "prop to occupy my time." In an interview with *Musician* shortly after the song's 1987 release, Stipe noted that the song is about "using people."

IT'S ABOUT SEX, NOT LOVE

The kind of girl who is impressed by the kind of guy who breaks out an acoustic guitar at a party is the kind of girl who loves Extreme's "More Than Words," which is the kind of song played by the kind of guy who breaks out an acoustic guitar at a party to impress a girl. It may sound sweet and romantic, but Extreme singer-songwriter Gary Cherone told VH1 that he wrote it from the point of view of a woman frustrated by her emotionless, romantic gesture—averse boyfriend, and how she wishes he would do something more grand and powerful beyond words . . . like playing her "More Than Words" on an acoustic guitar, for example.

IT'S ABOUT STALKING, NOT ROMANCE

Another favorite of assholes with acoustic guitars is "Crash Into Me," the pretty ballad that got the Dave Matthews Band a ton of mainstream attention in 1996. But just because it's slow and driven by an acoustic guitar doesn't make it a love song. Matthews said on his episode of *VH1 Storytellers*, in which songwriters explicitly admit what their songs are about, that "Crash Into Me" was written from the perspective "of a Peeping Tom" watching a girl at night through her bedroom window. The lyrics also command a woman to pull up her skirt and show off the goods, which sounds kind of rapey.

IT'S ABOUT ANARCHY AND ATHEISM, NOT WORLD PEACE

In "Imagine," his most famous and cherished song, and the one that serves as a shorthand legacy, John Lennon actually posits that the quickest way to world peace is to eliminate the twin oppressors of humanity: political boundaries and religion. While the message of dreaming about a peaceful world in the abstract was not lost on the millions of people who loved the song, the means with which to do it was. Lennon finally stated in a 1980 interview with *Playboy* (one of his last), that, like his "Give Peace a Chance," "Imagine" merely suggested that thinking about peace in "a world without countries or religion" was "positive."

<< >>

Here are four stories in which a record company executive told an artist that they "needed a single," the artist recorded a highly commercial single mocking the executive and their audacious request, and how that single became a hit, thus proving the executive absolutely correct when they said,

"We Don't Hear a Single"

WEEZER, "Pork and Beans" (2008)

Prior to the release of Weezer's self-titled 2008 album ("The Red Album"), Geffen Records executives heard a rough cut of it and told front man Rivers Cuomo to write more "commercial" stuff, which was pretty bewildering to Cuomo, considering the band's extensive catalog of super-catchy power pop. "I came out of it pretty angry," Cuomo told *Rolling Stone*. "But ironically, it inspired me to write another song." Cuomo composed "Pork and Beans," with sarcastic lyrics subtly dismissive of his label's criticism, and its want for catchy choruses and danceable beats. In the chorus, Cuomo asserts that he's "gonna do the things" that he wants to do, except that he didn't do the things he wanted to do. Because he wrote "Pork and Beans." The song was the album's first single, and with 11 weeks at #1 on *Billboard*'s Modern Rock Tracks chart, it's far and away the biggest hit Weezer has ever had.

LISA LOEB, "I Do" (1997)

Toward the end of recording *Firecracker*, Geffen executives, once again, listened to a rough cut and told Loeb that it had no marketable single. So, as Loeb wrote in the liner notes of her greatest hits album, "I decided to write a song that sounded like a song about a relationship but was actually about the record company not 'hearing' a single." The chorus and title refer to how the executives can't hear the accessible music, but *she* does. And indeed, they were deaf enough not to know the song was about the conversation they'd just had with Loeb. Still, "I Do," the leadoff single from *Firecracker*, made it to #17 on the *Billboard* Hot 100.

MAROON 5, "Harder to Breathe" (2002)

On first listen, "Harder to Breathe" is another misogynistic kiss-off from notorious poonhound and Maroon 5 lead singer Adam Levine degrading some supermodel he's grown bored of nailing. It's not. It's about Levine degrading the record company he's grown frustrated with trying to please. While working on Maroon 5's *Songs About Jane*, Levine was told by A&M Records that it lacked a marketable single. Levine, deeply confused because he was in one of the most openly commercial and middle-of-the-road bands in the history of recorded sound, got so mad that he and bandmate Jesse

ABOUT A SONG   43

Carmichael wrote "Harder to Breathe." Sample lyrics: "How dare you say that my behavior is unacceptable / So condescending, unnecessarily critical." Once more, the record company had no idea that it was being mocked and loved the song, releasing it as the first single from *Songs About Jane*. It went to #18 in the United States, proving A&M's corporate goons right. But Levine was right to be frustrated, as the album had plenty of potential hits. "This Love" and "She Will Be Loved," did even better than "Harder to Breathe," both reaching the *Billboard* top 5.

SARA BAREILLES, "Love Song" (2008)

The lead-up story is virtually the same as all the others: Singer/songwriter/pianist Sara Bareilles was signed to Epic and was recording her major-label debut *Little Voice* in 2007. Once Epic's A&R department heard *Little Voice* and realized it was sub–Michelle Branch pabulum, they ordered Bareilles to write some kind of catchy single, preferably a "love song." Pissed off she had to write bad music, or at least bad music that wasn't her idea, Bareilles wrote the wry, angry "Love Song" as a direct call-out to the record company. The first line of the chorus is literally, "I'm not gonna write you a love song." Epic paid no attention to the lyrics or intent, merely the title, and were pleased enough to release "Love Song" as Bareilles's first single. The song became a massive hit, making it to #4 on the *Billboard* Hot 100 in early 2008. But the only reason the song ever became a hit is because it reached a wide audience in a heavily aired TV commercial for Rhapsody, a music downloading service. Bareilles herself appeared in the commercial, performing the song live. Because that's how you show your record label that you aren't their little singing monkey: by being their little singing monkey.

Many musicians did not originate their signature songs. They may have popularized or perfected them, but they're still covers of obscure songs. Fortunately, for the original artist, there are songwriting royalties. Let's now all of us go

Under the Covers

GEORGE HARRISON, "Got My Mind Set on You"

Harrison had an out-of-nowhere comeback in 1987 fueled by this killer pop song. But Harrison, one of the best songwriters of all time (responsible for the Beatles' "Something," "What Is Life," and part of "My Sweet Lord"), didn't write this. Even though it's such a distinctively '80s kind of song, it was originated in the 1960s by an obscure soul singer named James Ray. Harrison had wanted to do the song back in the day with the Beatles, but he couldn't get his bandmates on board. Though Harrison admitted at the time that it wasn't a very well-put-together song, it at least had some good lyrics. He added in some synthy-sounding drums and removed from the original—as he described them in an interview with *Billboard*'s Fred Bronson—"horrible screechy women's voices singing backup parts."

ROBERTA FLACK, "Killing Me Softly with His Song"

The titular manly troubadour capable of felling and bedding a maiden with only the virtue of his sweet, sweet baritone: Don McLean. In 1971, singer Lori Lieberman saw McLean perform and she was so moved, in particular by the song "Empty Chairs," that she immediately went home and wrote a poem called "Killing Me Softly with His Blues." Lieberman took it to her friends, songwriters Charles Fox and Norman Gimbel, who wrote music for it (since a song about a musician made more sense than a poem about music) and changed "Blues" to "Song." Lieberman recorded it, but it didn't catch on with radio. Roberta Flack, however, heard Lieberman in, of all places, an in-flight recorded program. Simply because she liked the title, Flack recorded it. She took it to #1. Don McLean, meanwhile, is still performing the concert attended by Lori Lieberman in 1971, where he is about a third of the way through "American Pie."

DIONNE WARWICK AND FRIENDS, "That's What Friends Are For"

Carole Bayer Sager and Burt Bacharach wrote "That's What Friends Are For" to play over the end credits of the underrated 1982 Michael Keaton comedy *Night Shift*. It was sung by Rod Stewart, and despite him being Rod Stewart with His Inexplicably Enduring Popularity and Grating Smarminess, he couldn't make it a hit. In 1985, it was recorded by Dionne Warwick and Friends and became a smash #1 hit, its success buoyed by guilting the public into buying the 45—it was a charity single to benefit AIDS research. (The "Friends" were Elton John, Stevie Wonder, and Gladys Knight, so maybe that had something to do with the success.)

JOAN JETT, "I Love Rock 'n' Roll"

The Arrows, a 1970s English pop band, originated "I Love Rock 'n' Roll." It never charted in the United States, but Joan Jett made it her definitive song simply by switching the genders of the song's characters. And for some reason, a woman lusting after a 17-year-old guy seems a lot less creepy than a man lusting after a 17-year-old girl, or maybe we're all just too afraid of Joan Jett to say anything.

THEY MIGHT BE GIANTS, "Istanbul (Not Constantinople)"

The eccentric band's best-known song is certainly representative of their singular style, as weird instrumentation, clever wordplay, and esoteric references to academic subject matter are all present. But "Istanbul" was first performed by the Four Lads, a Canadian crooning quartet, who made a glacially slow, finger-snapping version a #10 hit in 1952.

TONI BASIL, "Mickey"

The British power pop band Racey released a song called "Kitty" in 1979. Sung by Racey's male lead singer Phil Fursdon, the object of the song was a girl—a girl named

Kitty. The final product sounded almost exactly like that year's biggest hit, the Knack's "My Sharona." And yet it was unsuccessful. But in 1981, choreographer and actress Toni Basil was cutting her debut album and decided to rewrite and cover "Kitty," switching the gender of the song's subject to a boy, renaming him Mickey after her real-life longtime crush: Micky Dolenz of the Monkees. Basil's version went all the way to #1. (She never did get any of that sweet Monkee love.)

JANIS JOPLIN, "Me and Bobby McGee"

It's Janis Joplin's signature song, probably because it was one of the few songs that fit her sometimes whiny, sometimes scratchy, sometimes off-key, always idiosyncratic voice. And it's pretty well known that Kris Kristofferson wrote it in his badass country music songwriter drifter phase, before he got all up in Barbra Streisand and the Nashville sound. Kristofferson wrote it from a male point of view, though (Bobby is a gender-neutral name, so no awkward sex-altering lyric changes were necessary for Joplin), and sought a male singer for it. The first person to record "Me and Bobby McGee" was old-time country stalwart Roger Miller.

NATALIE IMBRUGLIA, "Torn"

In 1998, an Australian soap star and former model named Natalie Imbruglia came out of nowhere with "Torn," a melancholy song with challenging lyrics, surprising choices for a supermodel's pop debut. Imbruglia didn't write the song, of course, nor did she have the foresight to select it or originate it. She was the fourth woman to sing it. It was written in 1991 by American songwriters Anne Preven, Phil Thornalley, and Scott Cutler, then translated into Danish, then sung by Danish superstar Lis Sørensen in 1993. It was then performed in English for the first time by Norwegian singer Trine Rein, where it was a top 10 hit (in Norway). Next, Preven and Cutler recorded it themselves in 1995, having recently formed the pop-punk band Ednaswap. Their version, sung by Preven, was not a hit in the United States (or Norway), but it was when RCA Records dug deep and commissioned it for the debut album by Imbruglia, 1998's *Left of the Middle*. Her version ended up one of the biggest hits of the decade, having been the most played song on American radio for 14 weeks.

YOUNGBLOODS, "Let's Get Together"

"Let's Get Together" was written in 1960 by Greenwich Village folkie Chet Powers (also known as Gino Valenti, and later a member of Quicksilver Messenger Service). He recorded a demo himself and tried to get the song a proper release, but to no avail in the pre-hippie '60s. Fellow folkies the Kingston Trio released a live version in 1964, but it wasn't a hit, nor was it for David Crosby, Jefferson Airplane, or Judy Collins. The Youngbloods took a stab at it in 1967, and it did okay, reaching #62 on the pop chart. But two years later, after the song was repeatedly used in PSAs promoting peace, brotherhood, and other hippie ideals faintly remembered today, it hit #5. From then on, it became an iconic flower-child anthem, mostly after the fact, popping up in countless

'60s documentaries, '60s-set movies, Boomer-targeted soda commercials, and what felt like every other episode of *China Beach*.

As filmmakers gave us things like *Ghostbusters 2* and *House Party 4*, so too have musicians crafted

Sequels to Songs

in order to similarly corrupt, complicate, and ruin things we once loved.

"SPACE ODDITY"

David Bowie introduced the Major Tom character in his first hit single, "Space Oddity." He's an astronaut floating through space until he loses contact with Ground Control, then floats around in oblivion, presumably forever. However, the song is allegorical. Like all '60s and '70s songs about space, it's really about drugs. Major Tom losing contact and drifting away is about losing contact with reality and becoming a hopeless, strung-out junkie. Bowie makes this literally and abundantly clear on his 1980 hit "Ashes to Ashes," where he bluntly states in as many words that Major Tom is a junkie.

"MAJOR TOM (COMING HOME)"

Well, German singer Peter Schilling didn't quite get the metaphor of "Space Oddity" nor the direct, outright statements of "Ashes to Ashes," and in 1983 released

"Major Tom (Coming Home)," a sequel to "Space Odd-ity" in that it takes the drifting astronaut plot literally and ignores "Ashes to Ashes" altogether. Ultimately, according to Schilling's song, the Major makes one last request, to tell his wife he loves her (echoing a lyric in "Space Oddity"), before he floats away into space for-ever, where luckily for him and unbeknownst to Schil-ling, there's plenty of room to do drugs and listen to David Bowie's awesome late '70s "Berlin Trilogy."

"UNEASY RIDER" (1973)

Fiddle-wizard Charlie Daniels ("The Devil Went Down to Georgia") was once part of the "rebel country" move-ment, a group that had more in common with the values (and gritty appearances) of the hippie counterculture than it did with the conservative South usually associ-ated with country music. (Daniels himself had worked in San Francisco with the Grateful Dead, so he was bona fide.) Daniels, born in the South, came down on the hippies' side with "Uneasy Rider" (1973), a sympathetic song sung from the point of view of a hippie who gets a flat tire outside a redneck bar in Jackson, Mississippi.

Some scary guys harass the hippie and force him to tip his hat to a skeezy old drunk lady, which causes all his long hippie hair to fall out of his hat. The rednecks laugh at the hippie, and so, as if with something to prove on his first day in prison, the peacenik kicks one of the rednecks in the knee, then tells the redneck's friends that the redneck is a secret liberal Communist homo-sexual on assignment from the FBI to take down the

Ku Klux Klan. And then the hippie gets the hell out of town.

"UNEASY RIDER '88"

By 1988, Daniels, like a lot of '60s counterculture types, had grown more conservative in his beliefs, so he wrote a sequel to "Uneasy Rider" called "Uneasy Rider '88." This time, the protagonist isn't a hippie starting trouble before anybody can mess with him, but two rednecks who stumble into a gay bar and end up starting a massive fight when one of them gay fellers makes a sexy move on them. So basically: In the first "Uneasy Rider," the hero is a guy Daniels identifies with that makes a violent, pre-emptive attack out of a pompous air of superiority and a fear of a strange place. In "Uneasy Rider '88," the heroes are *two guys* who Daniels identify with that make a violent, preemptive attack out of a pompous air of superiority and a fear of a strange place (and also of fellers kissing other fellers).

"IT'S MY PARTY"

Lesley Gore's "It's My Party" is a histrionic hissy fit of a teen pop song about a birthday party gone just tragically awry. The narrator's boyfriend, Johnny, of course, as all boys in the late '50s/early '60s were named, comes to his girlfriend/narrator's birthday party, but leaves with—*gasp*—some slut named Judy, even—*gasp*—giving her his class ring. The narrator then cries and cries and cries. But hey, you would cry too if it happened to you, because it's the worst thing that's ever happened in the history of the world. The song, one of the first ever produced by Quincy Jones, was a #1 smash in the summer of 1963, unseating the even more embarrassingly dated and sexist "If You Wanna Be Happy" by Jimmy Soul. (That song tells us to never marry pretty women, because attractive ladies lead to misery, or something.)

"JUDY'S TURN TO CRY"

"It's My Party" sort of leaves things open-ended; there are scores of untapped soapy teenage drama still left to mine. While the song was still rising on the charts, Gore went back to the studio and recorded a sequel, "Judy's Turn to Cry," so the world would no longer be in suspense over what became of the whiny narrator, that cad Johnny, and Judy, the goddamn whore. And so, in "Judy's Turn to Cry," the three characters are at another swell boy-girl party with dancing, soda pop, and adult supervision when the narrator kisses some poor, random, unwitting pawn of a boy to make Johnny jealous. Johnny, there with that smug skank Judy, notices the kiss and goes and punches the innocent boy. Johnny then professes to our unlovable narrator that he *does* love her after all and they get back together. And then, it's Judy's turn to cry. Unfortunately, the story ends there, with a happy reunion of two self-absorbed teenagers who are just *perfect* for each other. Never recorded was a song from the point of view of the narrator's nameless date, which might have been titled "First She Kissed Me (Then I Got Punched) and Then I Cried, Too."

When a crap song hits #1, it doesn't necessarily mean that millions of people all love the song; it's that a few hundred thousand people liked it just barely enough to all buy the single, all at some point during the same seven-day period. Once in a while, enough people like something weird just barely enough all at the same time, and these songs become

The Unlikeliest #1 Hits Ever

SOEUR SOURIRE (THE SINGING NUN),
"Dominique" (1963)

Jeanne Deckers was born in Belgium in 1933 and joined a convent in 1954, where she adopted the name Sister Luc-Gabrielle and entertained the other nuns with songs about saints she wrote and played on the acoustic guitar. (There wasn't a lot to do in Belgian convents in the 1950s.) The head nuns thought she should record and distribute her songs as a way to spread the word of God, and earn money for the convent, so they booked time to record them professionally at the Philips Studio in Brussels. Philips executives loved the songs, signed Deckers/Sister Luc-Gabrielle to a contract, and renamed her Soeur Sourire (French for "Sister Smile"). The first single released was "Dominique," a lilting folk song, sung in French, about Saint Dominic (founder of the Dominican order and the patron saint of astronomers . . . but you know that). Inexplicably, "Dominique" was a massive hit across Europe, so Philips released it in the United States in late 1963, where in the wake of the Kennedy assassination, radio programmers were eschewing rock and Motown in favor of soft, happy easy listening-type songs to pacify the freaked-out populace. To recap: a song sung in French by a Belgian nun about a thirteenth-century Catholic saint was a #1 song for four weeks in the United States well after the introduction of the devil's music.

KYU SAKAMOTO, "Sukiyaki" (1963)

A song sung in Japanese by a Japanese singer made it to #1 in an era of American history in which the common perception of the Japanese was somewhere in between kamikaze pilot and Mickey Rooney's portrayal of a bucktoothed *Chinaman* in *Breakfast at Tiffany's*. "Sukiyaki" is a catchy, cryptic, mid-tempo ballad performed melodramatically from the point of view of a man who is sad and heartbroken at best, or on his way to the executioner at worst. It was a massive hit in 1961 in Japan by Kyu Sakamoto under its real title, "Ue o muite aruko"—roughly, "I Look Up When I Walk." Louis Benjamin, an executive at the British label Pye Records, heard it on an Asian vacation and secured the rights for it to be performed as an instrumental by the British group Kenny Ball and His Jazzmen. In a woeful and extreme act of cultural belittlement, the foreign-sounding title was changed to "Sukiyaki" to make it more familiar to white audiences, *sukiyaki* being a Japanese entrée consisting of beef and rice, popular at the time. The Ball version was a major hit in the United Kingdom and a curious DJ in eastern Washington who liked it dug up Sakamoto's original and played it . . . and the song spread across the United States. Capitol Records got the rights from Pye to release the song Stateside, retaining the ridiculous "Sukiyaki" title, and it amazingly shot to #1. Sakamoto never had another hit in the United States, probably because most Americans were not yet familiar with enough Japanese things that could have been used for song titles. If "Ue o muite aruko" were released today, under the same "familiar Japanese thing"-naming concept, it would be dubbed "Hello Kitty Sushi Godzilla Bento Box Michelle Kwan."

HUGH MASEKELA, "Grazing in the Grass" (1968)

"Grazing in the Grass" is an instrumental jazz tune by Masekela, a South African trumpet player. A cover version of the song—with lyrics—released a year later by the Friends of Distinction is better known, appearing in movies such as *Anchorman* (during the "cannonball!" scene) and *I'm Gonna Git You Sucka*. That brassed-up version went to #3 in 1969 and it is a representative joyful soul hit of the era, but the original is much slower, and is basically a combination of Masekela's trumpet and a frantic ringing of cowbells. And while that is the one that few remember, it's the one that actually topped the chart a year earlier in 1968.

CHUCK BERRY, "My Ding-a-Ling" (1972)

Chuck Berry didn't invent rock 'n' roll music, but he might as well have. Unfairly, the only #1 hit of his career

is this ridiculous tune. Consisting entirely of Berry pluck-
ing out the notes one-by-one on a guitar while a live audience sings backup, it's a novelty song built on the double
entendre of how talking about a yo-yo could be mistaken
for talking about a penis. That kind of thing can get some
attention for a couple days (especially on wacky morning
radio and elementary school playgrounds), but the fact
that for a period of time, scores of Americans said, "Hello,
record store clerk. Here is my hard-earned money. One
copy of 'My Ding-a-Ling' please," boggles the mind.

THE EDGAR WINTER GROUP, "Frankenstein" (1973)

This is an instrumental hard rock song performed by
an albino guitar whiz who instead of playing the guitar
mostly plays a synthesizer. Although "Frankenstein" pioneered the use of the keytar, there was never before, nor
ever again, a synth-driven hard rock song without lyrics
to top the chart. (No albinos ever hit #1 again either.)

JAMES BLUNT, "You're Beautiful" (2006)

In the mid-'00s (pronounced "oughts"), hip-hop absolutely dominated pop music. In the two years before
this song peaked in March 2006, only two non-hip-
hop/R&B songs had made it to #1: Both were *American
Idol* finale songs, and both were there for a single, per-
functory week each. James Blunt's plodding, simplistic,
Clay Aiken-on-Quaaludes ballad as if sung by a prepubescent Bee Gee somehow made it to the top of the
charts in the United States. And in an age where looks
matter, "You're Beautiful" was released by a singer that

looks like Napoleon Dynamite. Not Jon Heder, the actor, but the character, Napoleon Dynamite.

LORNE GREENE, "Ringo" (1964)

During the 1964–65 TV season, the most watched TV show in the United States was the western *Bonanza*. It produced a heartthrob teen idol sensation in costar Michael Landon, but he wasn't the one with the hit record. *Bonanza* star Lorne Greene—49-year-old stone-faced, monotone-delivering Canadian actor Lorne Greene—recorded "Ringo," a spoken-to-music story song about an Old West gunfighter of the same name. Perhaps it had something to do with the Beatlemania that dominated pop culture in 1964 that even a spoken word record about the Old West sung by an aging, uncharismatic character actor could be a smash hit if it had the name of a Beatle in the title.

U2 has created many enduring classics, such as "With or Without You," and "One," and Bono should be lauded for his tireless humanitarian efforts. But U2 only makes so many timeless, haunting love songs. For the most part, U2 records songs about

Whatever Social Ill U2 Was Upset About That Day

"THE ELECTRIC CO." (1980): Before U2 could take on the problems of the world, they had to start small, and start with what they knew, and that was Ireland. This song off their first album *Boy*, their first social protest song, rails against electroshock therapy, which at the time was still a common treatment in Irish mental hospitals.

"SUNDAY BLOODY SUNDAY" (1983): The January 1972 massacre of 13 Irish people by British troops at a civil rights protest in Northern Ireland is known throughout Ireland as Bloody Sunday, and that's what "Sunday Bloody Sunday" is about. It's also a call for peace; Bono used to wave a giant white flag in live performances of the song.

"PEACE ON EARTH" (2000): It's also about the conflict in Northern Ireland, going so far as to include a list of names of people killed in a 1998 IRA bombing.

"VAN DIEMEN'S LAND" (1988): The title is what nineteenth-century Europeans called the Australian island of Tasmania, initially a British penal colony. The Edge, who wrote the song, dedicated this *Rattle and Hum* track to John Boyle O'Reilly, an Irish nationalist poet so thoroughly an Irish nationalist that the British banished him to Van Diemen's Land in 1867.

"WHERE THE STREETS HAVE NO NAME" (1987): While rumored to be about Bono's trip to a famine-ravaged Ethiopia, the singer divulged in a fan club newsletter that it's actually a treatise on the social divides of Irish cities, specifically Belfast, where neighborhoods are clearly delineated by both economic class and religion.

"RED HILL MINING TOWN" (1987): In 1984, Bono met Bob Dylan when the latter played a show in Dublin, inspiring the former to learn more about American folk music, which he discovered often had a lefty political bent. Around the same time, mine workers were on strike in the United Kingdom, and so Bono wrote this lefty political song as a show of solidarity for the miners.

"THE PLAYBOY MANSION" (1997): In short, it argues that America is a materialistic place, and the decadent Playboy Mansion is both a perfect example and microcosm of this. (This might be a good time to mention that Bono started wearing shades and a leather jacket to portray a character called the Fly, a sleazy, clichéd rock star, as part of the early '90s Zoo TV stage show. Bono then pretty much adopted the shades and leather jacket as his permanent uniform, removing the Fly of all its satire and Bono of a good chunk of his credibility.)

"EVEN BETTER THAN THE REAL THING" (1991): Bono thinks that we've all grown so shortsighted and materialistic that we don't care about genuine, lasting experiences anymore. "Living in the present, in the now—and not looking to what's around the corner," Bono says in regards to the song in Niall Stokes's *U2: Into the Heart*, "is very dangerous politically, ecologically, in relationships, to the family. But that's where people are at right now." Moreover, the title is a play on Coca-Cola's "The Real Thing" slogan, leading Richard Branson to ask U2 to use the song in ads for his Coke competitor Virgin Cola. They declined.

"CRUMBS FROM YOUR TABLE" (2004): An extension of Bono's ongoing efforts to get the world's wealthiest nations to forgive third-world debt (initially via the Jubilee 2000 organization), the song details how Bono feels that while it's all well and good that the rich countries of the world do give aid to the poor countries of the world, it's still relatively nothing, or "crumbs."

"PRIDE (IN THE NAME OF LOVE)" (1984): This is a tribute to Martin Luther King—his murder is both mentioned and dramatized in the song.

"WALK ON" (2000): According to the liner notes from *All That You Can't Leave Behind*, it's a tribute to Aung San Suu Kyi, a Burmese activist and politician who stood up to her country's oppressive military regime in 1988, and was placed under house arrest for most of the next 20 years, until she was finally freed in November 2010.

"NEW YEAR'S DAY" (1983): Bono has told reporters that as he was recording this song in 1982—conceived as a nontraditional love song—he was thinking a lot about Solidarity, a labor union movement in Poland led by Lech Walesa that represented one of the first blows to the authority of that country's Communist government (which Walesa would ultimately help topple completely by decade's end). Bono says that as he sung the song, an image appeared in his head—that of Walesa standing in the snow, leading an employment strike.

"STRANGER IN A STRANGE LAND" (1981): Bono said in the *Zoo TV* concert film that it was inspired by a lonely border guard the band met on a trip to East Berlin.

"SILVER AND GOLD" (1988): It's a condemnation of apartheid, which the band recorded for the anti-apartheid awareness/benefit album *Sun City*.

"BULLET THE BLUE SKY" (1987): Bono wanted *The Joshua Tree* to be an album about the disparity in the concept and execution of "America" (page 8) and, as reported in Bill Flanagan's *U2: At the End of the World*, he needed to go see "the worst side of the American Dream." So the band went to El Salvador in 1986, where they learned firsthand about the United States' Central American policy under Ronald Reagan, which consisted of giving weapons and money to crazy guerilla groups, so long as they were overthrowing Communist governments. Bono wrote some aggressive lyrics, then told the Edge to "put El Salvador through your amplifier."

"MOTHERS OF THE DISAPPEARED" (1987): In the 1970s, critics of the military regime that governed Argentina had a way of disappearing forever. These victims came to be known as "The Disappeared."

"GET ON YOUR BOOTS" (2009): Bono told reporters during press for the *No Line on the Horizon* album that "get on your boots" is East African slang for "put on a condom." In other words, it's a call for safe sex to stem the African AIDS crisis.

"LOVE AND PEACE OR ELSE" (2004): That's a pretty self-evident title. But yeah, it's about how war is bad, particularly the never-ending fight over Israel.

"TRYIN' TO THROW YOUR ARMS AROUND THE WORLD" (1991): In what is perhaps the most breathtaking bit of irony in the history of popular music, the U2 song called "Tryin' to Throw Your Arms Around the World" is not about social ills or the burden of curing them. Bono introduced this one on stage during the Zoo TV tour as, simply, "a drinking song," and as such would bring a fan up onstage to share a glass of champagne.

I get pretty frustrated when I ask somebody what their favorite band is and they tell me that it's the Beatles. I mean, of course you like the Beatles. Everybody likes the Beatles. What I meant was, who *besides* the Beatles is your favorite band? Liking the Beatles isn't interesting or unique. But the Britpop band Oasis doesn't see anything wrong with famously cramming its works with Beatles allusions, collected here in

A Children's Garden of Beatles References in the Works of Oasis

"DON'T LOOK BACK IN ANGER"

Noel Gallagher claims he came into possession of a bootleg tape of John Lennon's memoir dictation. In talking about the "bed-in" protests of 1969, Lennon mentions that he "was trying to start a revolution from my bed," which became a prominent lyric in Oasis's 1996 hit "Don't Look Back in Anger."

The song's opening piano riff is just similar enough to the one from John Lennon's "Imagine" to make you think of "Imagine," but different enough so as to avoid litigation. But if it's too different, it might have been an accident, because in a lengthy segment about the band's penchant for riff-borrowing in the 1996 documentary *Oasis: Mad For It*, Gallagher states bluntly that "in the case of 'Don't Look Back in Anger,' the opening piano riff *is* 'Imagine.'"

"WONDERWALL"

The song was originally titled "Wishing Stone," but Liam Gallagher ultimately called it "Wonderwall," more or less a nonsense word in the context of the song, but inspired by the 1968 film *Wonderwall*. The soundtrack to that movie was a bunch of songs written and performed by George Harrison.

"SUPERSONIC"

Heading hilariously into lyrics about the need to be original and true to oneself, the song's lead guitar riff is structurally and melodically similar to the riff from George Harrison's classic "My Sweet Lord." This homage is quite meta—Harrison was successfully sued for subconsciously plagiarizing elements of "My Sweet Lord" from the Chiffons' 1963 pop hit "He's So Fine."

Moreover, a lyric in "Supersonic" mentions a yellow submarine, which is of course an allusion to "Penny Lane."

"SHAKERMAKER"

The main melody was taken from "I'd Like to Teach the World to Sing (in Perfect Harmony)," the 1970 folk song/Coke jingle as performed by the New Seekers, at least according to a court of law. The songwriters sued Oasis for appropriating the tune, and Oasis had to pay $500,000 (Australian, where the New Seekers were from) in damages. Gallagher remained adamant that he didn't steal from "I'd Like to Teach the World to Sing," because, as he told *Addicted to Noise* in 1995, his writing process for "Shakermaker" had been to "just put lyrics to 'Flying,'" an instrumental track from the Beatles' *Magical Mystery Tour*.

"ALL AROUND THE WORLD"

In the song's reprise, the chord progression and backing vocal is a near replica of the one from "Hey Jude." There's even an ever-louder brass band in the mix, just like in "Hey Jude." Also, the video for the song is animated. The band travels around a crazy, psychedelic world in a yellow . . . spaceship.

"THE MASTERPLAN"

This time, Oasis drops all pretense. Near the end of the song—about 30 seconds left or so—Noel Gallagher just straight up sings the chorus of "Octopus's Garden."

OASIS

Manchester-based Oasis took its name from a home-town club where the Beatles played in 1963.

THE GODDAMN DRUMMER

In the ultimate Oasis tribute to the Beatles, in 2004 drummer Alan White quit and was replaced with Zak Starkey, whose father is Richard Starkey, better known as Ringo Starr.

Fun fact: 75 percent of classic rock songs are about Pattie Boyd, a captivating British model and one-time wife of George Harrison. All right, so not *that* many. But a lot, including

"Layla," and Other Assorted Love Songs About George Harrison's Wife

The Beatles did everything in rock first, including marrying models. George's wife Pattie Boyd was the hottest Beatle wife (with Ringo's wife Barbara Bach a close second), but only the second-most interesting Beatle wife (she's a distant second to Yoko). Boyd and Harrison met in 1964 when the 19-year-old was cast as a screaming fan in *A Hard Day's Night*. They married two years later. Harrison was already a great songwriter, but Boyd became his muse, inspiring some of his best songs.

"WHAT IS LIFE," a joyous rocker from his solo master-piece *All Things Must Pass*, for example, celebrates Boyd.

Being both married and having classic songs written about her would seemingly put Boyd off the market, but not if you're Mick Jagger or John Lennon. Each tried to seduce Boyd on several occasions. Boyd turned them both down, but she did have an affair with Ronnie Wood of the Faces and the Rolling Stones. Wood and Harrison were friends, and when Wood was staying at Harrison's house one night in 1977, he boldly informed the Beatle that when night fell, he'd be sleeping with Boyd. Nonplussed, Harrison slept with Wood's wife, Krissie. Wives? Swapped. At least for the night. Wood went on to write **"BREATHE ON ME"** and **"MYSTIFIES ME"** about Boyd.

Needless to say, there were some marital tensions. Boyd ended up confiding her problems (such as Harrison's endless, shameless carousing) to Harrison's long-time best friend who was always hanging around: Eric Clapton. All that emotional intensity led Clapton to fall in love with Boyd, but lacking the balls of third-string British rock star *Ronnie Wood*, Clapton didn't think he could do anything about it. So, when he was in Derek and the Dominoes, he wrote **"LAYLA,"** a song of anguished, forbidden love. (It's named after "The Story of Layla," an ancient Persian poem about unrequited love.) Harrison's constant infidelity drove Boyd to divorce him in 1977. "Layla," which Clapton had written and recorded in 1970, finally worked, after nine years: In 1979, Boyd and Clapton married.

While they were involved (but not yet married),

Clapton and Boyd were getting ready to go out one night. They'd been invited to Paul and Linda McCartney's annual Buddy Holly–themed party. (Rock star critical mass for this story has now been reached.) Clapton was frustrated by how long it was taking Boyd to get ready and wrote **"WONDERFUL TONIGHT."** It's not a sweet love song in which a guy tells his wife how beautiful she looks; he's saying, "You look fine, come on, let's *go*! All the best cocaine is gonna be gone by the time we get there!"

In addition to "Wonderful Night," other songs Clapton wrote about Boyd (before and while he had her) include **"BELL BOTTOM BLUES," "PRETTY BLUE EYES," "GOLDEN RING," "PRETTY GIRL,"** and the ultimately false **"NEVER MAKE YOU CRY."** Clapton's drug problems and infidelity led Boyd to divorce him in 1988. Boyd has yet to remarry, but when she does it'll probably be to one of the Kinks, the only major '60s British rock band her mystique didn't infiltrate.

And while it's common knowledge that Harrison wrote the moving Beatles love song "Something" about Boyd, it's not true. Harrison told *Undercover* magazine in 1996 that he was actually inspired by—and was thinking about, as he wrote it—the music that personally moved him, specifically that of Ray Charles. However, Boyd wrote in her autobiography *Wonderful Tonight* that Harrison told her it *was* about her, so at least he had enough good sense and wifely affection to let Boyd think that a composition Frank Sinatra called "the greatest love song of the past 50 years" was about her.

<< >>

Most duets are love songs, and if the performers can effectively sell it, the listener is to assume, or at least question, if'n the two singers are romantically involved, or, you know, bonin'. The truth of the matter is that sometimes the artists is bonin', sometimes they is not bonin', once in a while they wasn't bonin' anymore, and sometimes they was not yet bonin', but would be bonin' in the future. Whenever I hear a duet, I wonder,

So, Was They Bonin', or Was They Not Bonin'?

KENNY ROGERS AND DOLLY PARTON, "Islands in the Stream" (1983)

NOT BONIN'. Despite these two being more inseparable in the '80s than Ronald Reagan and his doting mother Nancy, and the fact that most children at the time thought that they were married (at least I did), no bonin' here. Parton has been with her rarely seen husband Carl Dean since 1966. Rogers has had five wives, none of them were Dolly, a fact that likely haunts him as he lays awake each night, weeping facedown on a pair of gigantic pillows as he screams, "*You're* the coward of the county, Kenny Rogers. *You are.* For letting *her* get away!"

STEVIE NICKS AND DON HENLEY,
"Leather and Lace" (1981)

NOT BONIN' ANYMORE. The song was made in 1981; Henley and Nicks dated off and on in the late '70s. Nicks stayed on good terms with Henley, which would mean he's easier to deal with than her other famous ex-beau, Fleetwood Mac bandmate Lindsey Buckingham. Still, Buckingham is a badass guitarist while Don Henley is a tool. **FUN BONUS FACTY FACT:** Henley told *GQ* in 1991 that the Fleetwood Mac song "Sara," written and sung by Nicks, is about an unborn daughter he made her abort. Nicks denies it, which possibly makes Henley arrogant to assume the song was somehow about him—the kind of guy that forces his girlfriend to get an abortion, and also the kind of guy who freely tells the world that he made his girlfriend get an abortion.

WHITNEY HOUSTON AND BOBBY BROWN,
"Something in Common" (1993)

BONIN'. They're now divorced, but Houston and Brown were married at the time of this incredibly sugary New Jack duet, a jab at people who said the good girl and bad boy had nothing in common. But then they made a forgettable song together, got hooked on drugs together, and went completely insane together, so there you go: lots in common after all.

PAULA ABDUL AND MC SKAT KAT,
"Opposites Attract" (1989)

NOT BONIN'. Rather than make sweet love to an animated rapping cat, Abdul chose to date Arsenio Hall, 1989's second funkiest cat in oversized purple pants.

JOHNNY CASH AND JUNE CARTER,
"Jackson" (1967)

NOT BONIN' YET. Carter and Cash were attracted to each other, but were involved with other people. A year after "Jackson," a song about a failing marriage, was released, the singers married.

HUMAN LEAGUE, "Don't You Want Me" (1981)

SORT OF BONIN'. This duet, which could be called "How Come We Don't Bone Anymore?" is sung by Human League front man Philip Oakey and backup singer Susan Ann Sulley. At the time, Oakey was bonin' the other backup singer in the band, Joanne Catherall.

BROOKS AND DUNN, "Boot Scootin' Boogie" (1992)

NOT BONIN'. Brooks was not bonin' Dunn, nor was Dunn bonin' Brooks. The lyric "get down, turn around, go to town," does not mean *that*. This is *country* music, people. In country music, bonin' is a serious, sacred bond between married, moderately related teenagers.

MARVIN GAYE AND KIM WESTON,
"It Takes Two" (1966)

NOT BONIN'. While Gaye would sometimes get a feeling that would require sexual healing, he didn't get any relief from Weston. Her husband, Mickey Stevenson, produced the track and probably would have noticed any bonin' in the recording booth.

PRINCE AND SHEENA EASTON,
"U Got the Look" (1987)

BONIN'. Well, probably. It is Prince and he boned most of his protégés, Easton included. Scientific fact: In the '80s, Prince was bonin' two out of every three ladies on Earth, usually at the same time.

ASHFORD AND SIMPSON, "Solid" (1984)

BONIN'. While songwriters at Motown Records, Nick Ashford and Valerie Simpson wrote classic duets like "Ain't No Mountain High Enough," "Ain't Nothing Like the Real Thing," and other songs that didn't piss all over the rules of English grammar. As performers, "Solid" is their only well known hit. They've been romantically involved since the 1960s and married since 1974.

NATALIE COLE AND NAT "KING" COLE,
"Unforgettable" (1991)

NOT BONIN'. A duet between a cash-strapped, nostalgia-milking daughter and her computer-generated, long-dead father indicates that there was no bonin'. Fathers generally don't bone their daughters, especially if they are dead and/or robots.

ELTON JOHN AND KIKI DEE,
"Don't Go Breaking My Heart" (1976)

NOT BONIN'. According to some media reports, Elton John is a "homosexual."

CHER AND PETER CETERA, "After All" (1989)

NOT BONIN'. If'n they was bonin', it was, at best, phonin' bonin'. They weren't even in the studio together when the song was recorded. Cher and Man-Cher recorded their tracks separately, and they were spliced together later. So thanks for pioneering multitrack recording, Les Paul, which made forgettable duets by disinterested megastars possible.

GLORIA ESTEFAN AND *NSYNC,
"Music of My Heart" (1999)

NOT BONIN'. As hot as the prospect of a *ménage-a-six* sounds, the possibility is about as much of a reality as this mawkish, barely-there wisp of a song about inspirational music teachers. Of *NSYNC, Lance Bass is gay, Justin Timberlake only sleeps with *FHM* cover models, and Joey Fatone is gross.

CHAPTER 3

Band on the Run

ABOUT THE MUSICIANS AND SUCH

A Secret Identity

is an occasionally employed device for musicians who want to be clever or anonymous or cleverly anonymous (but not anonymously clever).

THE FIREMAN

One of the most critically acclaimed dance recordings of 1993 (inasmuch as a dance recording can be critically acclaimed) was *Strawberries Oceans Ships Forest*, an electronica album by an act called the Fireman. It also generated a handful of popular tracks in American dance clubs and European discotheques. The identity of the Fireman? It wasn't one person, but a duo made up of, surprisingly, Martin Glover of the pioneering goth group Killing Joke, and even more surprisingly, Paul McCartney. That damn Paul McCartney can be wildly successful at anything, even if it's electronica, and even when people don't necessarily know it's him, which I suppose means he's still got talent and can sell records beyond mere name recognition. But still, Paul—you're making the rest of us, but mostly Ringo, look bad.

THE MASKED MARAUDERS

Back in the '60s, *Rolling Stone* hadn't yet started mythologizing itself and everything that happened in the musical world between the years of 1956 and 1972. It actually once had a sense of humor about rock music and was even capable of taking the piss out of Baby Boomer icons. In October 1969, the magazine published a review by T. M. Christian of the self-titled release by a new band called the Masked Marauders. No names were listed on the mysterious album, Christian reported, but from the sounds of the voices on the record, it was obviously a supergroup made up of Mick Jagger, Bob Dylan, John Lennon, Paul McCartney, and George Harrison— basically the Traveling Wilburys minus Roy Orbison, Tom Petty, and Jeff Lynne (in other words, *pass*). *Rolling Stone*'s legions of Beatles- and Dylan-worshipping drones dutifully requested the album at record stores all over the country, but curiously couldn't find it anywhere. Even the most knowledgeable record store clerks (even back then they knew about every album ever made) had never heard of anything called the "Masked Marauders." That's because T.M. Christian wasn't real, and neither were the Masked Marauders. The whole thing had been a ruse by *Rolling Stone* staff writer Greil Marcus under a pseudonym (T. M. Christian is an allusion to fringe satirical author Terry Southern's novel *The Magic Christian*, made into a movie starring Ringo Starr the year this story takes place, with a soundtrack called *Magic Christian Music* recorded by Beatles protégé band Badfinger). Still, demand was so high for the album that Marcus hired a group called the Cleanliness and Godliness Skiffle Band to record the "real" Masked Marauders album. Marcus made a quick buck when it actually sold more than 100,000 copies, but upon listening to it, most people figured out the jig was up, owing to the studio band's terrible impersonations of Dylan (he's mumbly!) and McCartney (he's British!).

THE NETWORK

In September 2003, an electro/New Wave band called the Network released *Money Money 2020* on Adeline Records. Having made no public appearances or even registering a website up until a few weeks before the album came out made the Network something of a mystery. Also adding to the mystery was actual mystery—the band performed and was always photographed (including on the album cover) wearing masks, and band members' names and back stories were egregiously comical and over-the-top in their absurdity. Band leader Fink, for example, claimed to finance the band's operations with money earned from inventing a top-secret nuclear device at MIT, Van Gough was a Belgian macrobiotic vegan, and drummer the Snoo was a former Mexican wrestler from Argentina.

It was essentially a novelty act, but for some reason there was an instant and massive rivalry between this new group and the mega-popular band Green Day. "Just because you wrote 'Keep Them Separated,'" the

Network's manager, Doctor S., lashed out on the band's website, wryly confusing Green Day with its class of '94 new-punk cohorts the Offspring, "don't come screaming at us because we are young and hot. We're here to start a revolution, and either you are in or you are out." One of Green Day singer Billie Joe Armstrong's retorts: "All I gotta say is fuck the Network. These guys are totally spreading rumors." That rumor: that the Network was actually Green Day in secret, which Armstrong has vehemently denied.

So yeah, the Network was absolutely Green Day. Well, probably. (Okay, definitely.) Not only was the Network signed to Adeline Records, a label co-owned by Billie Joe Armstrong, but their masks weren't particularly concealing; take a glance at a few press photos and you can easily ascertain that Armstrong is Fink and drummer Tre Cool is the Snoo. (Bassist Mike Dirnt is Van Gough; Captain Underpants is guitarist Jason White.) Furthermore, a song by the Network was included on *Green Day: Rock Band*, and music publishing records show that the songwriters on *Money Money 2020* are Armstrong, Dirnt, and Cool.

CAMILLE

Prince is famously prolific, said to be hiding away thousands of hours of unreleased material. He's had almost as many female protégés, such as Vanity, Apollonia, and Sheila E. He had another one named "Camille." But while Prince's stocked vault may or may not exist, Camille most definitely did not. Prince is Camille. Using basic studio trickery, Prince sped up and pitch-shifted his voice so it sounded feminine, and in 1986 recorded (and then shelved) an entire album recorded as Camille. Camille (or the Camille technique) does, however, make a guest appearance on 1987's "U Got the Look" and she sings lead on Prince's single "If I Was Your Girlfriend." Perhaps Prince realized the whole ruse was completely unnecessary when he remembered that his voice isn't exactly a deep, rich, manly basso profondo.

ANN COATES

Like Prince, the Smiths created a fake female backup singer while recording "Bigmouth Strikes Again" in 1985. Morrissey took a recording of his harmony overdubs and sped it up until he had an extremely high voice, as if dosed with large amounts of helium. He named "her" Ann Coates, which is a play on Ancoats, Morrissey's home neighborhood in Manchester, England. Ann Coates is credited as background vocalist on *The Queen Is Dead*, where "Bigmouth Strikes Again" appeared.

MICHAEL JACKSON, "Mystery Girl"

Jackson's 1992 hit "In the Closet" was a duet on his *Dangerous* album about a love affair that must be always, always kept secret (which, as the prosecution would like to point out, was Jackson's preferred way to handle a relationship). To add to the song's inherent "mystery," the female singer on the song is identified in the *Dangerous* liner notes as "Mystery Girl." Who is Mystery Girl? Well, it sounds a lot like Janet Jackson, but it isn't, as that would have been too creepy, even for Michael

Jackson. And it's not supermodel Naomi Campbell, who stars in the "In the Closet" music video and lip syncs the lyrics, and who had a modest music career going at the time. The Mystery Girl is actually Princess Stephanie of Monaco, who was also attempting a pop career at the time. While she had the royal clout to get herself placed on a Michael Jackson single, she forgot to realize that a major part of marketing yourself is to tell your audience who you are.

It takes a lot of struggle over a long period of time to come up with a song that becomes a hit. And it's just as hard to get that second hit, and often that proves impossible. Thus is created a "one-hit wonder," and thus is created for the one-hit wonder cash flow problems. So what do they do? It's all part of

The Secret Lives of One-Hit Wonders

GERARDO, "Rico Suave" (#7 in 1991)

Gerardo ushered in the era of Latin rap with his song "Rico Suave," half rapped in Spanish, half rapped in English in a style Gerardo called "spanglish" (not to be confused with Adam Sandler's *Spanglish*). However, he was the *only* Latin rap act, as his lascivious pool boy/ extra-greasy Richard Grieco in acid-washed jeans act quickly wore thin. He released a few more albums of little distinction before signing on as an artists and repertoire guy (usually called "A&R," it's essentially a talent scout and developer) with Interscope Records in 1995. In 1998, he made the next Latin pop wave a reality: He signed Enrique Iglesias and supervised his 1998 English-language album.

RUPERT HOLMES, "Escape (The Piña Colada Song)" (#1 in 1979)

Holmes's career trajectory really isn't surprising, considering his hit was a quirky, fairly humorous, story song (the chick he hooked up with in the personal ads was his "lady," who was also evidently looking to cheat; they share a good laugh while avoiding an uncomfortable confrontation about mutual attempted adultery). He moved on to musical theatre, where he wrote the lyrics, music, and script for *The Mystery of Edwin Drood*, based on an unfinished Charles Dickens novel. It debuted on Broadway in 1985 and Holmes won two Tony Awards for it. He also wrote the novel *Where the Truth Lies*, about a faded comedy duo, which was made into a film in 2005.

4 NON BLONDES, "What's Up" (#14 in 1993)

In an era of New Jack Swing on pop radio, the scowling, screaming bohemians in floppy Dr. Seuss hats of 4 Non Blondes were a welcome if surprising addition to the top 40. It couldn't last, and lead singer and main songwriter Linda Perry became one of the most sought-after producers and writers in 2000s pop. She has worked mostly with female singers, both blond (Christina Aguilera, "Beautiful") and non-blond (Pink, "Get the Party Started").

C. W. MCCALL, "Convoy" (#1 in 1976)

In 1973, William Fries was working at Bozell and Jacobs, an Omaha advertising agency, where he designed a campaign for Metz, a regional bakery. The ads featured a character named C. W. McCall, a bread truck driver. They were so popular that "McCall" began recording songs (voiced by Fries), with lyrics written by Fries and the music written by Chip Davis, a jingle writer at Bozell and Jacobs. The most famous of those songs was "Convoy," a story song about three truckers talking on their CB radios, which kicked off the 1970s CB radio fad. While Fries sang on six albums of diminishing returns as McCall, Davis has had a massively successful recording career, although still under a pseudonym. He's the man behind Mannheim Steamroller, the synthesizer act that is best known for its Christmas albums. Davis, as the Steamroller, has sold a staggering 40 million albums, most of them to your mom.

MIDNIGHT OIL, "Beds Are Burning" (#17 in 1988)

"Beds Are Burning" is one of more than a dozen hits for Midnight Oil in its native Australia, but for most Americans, "Beds Are Burning" is the *only* Midnight Oil song. Lead singer Peter Garrett wrote it about the oppression of Australia's Aboriginal peoples; "Beds Are Burning" advocates giving ancestral land back to the indigenous Pintupi. It's not that shocking then that after the group broke up in 2002, Garrett went into politics. In 2004, he was elected to Australia's Parliament and in 2007 was appointed the Minister for the Environment, Heritage, and the Arts. He's like the Bono of Australia, only with actual power and responsibilities.

THOMAS DOLBY, "She Blinded Me with Science" (#5 in 1983)

Dolby is one of the main acts that brought electronic music into the mainstream, making him pretty much responsible for the whole of the glorious synth-heavy '80s pop that came after. Dolby himself only had the one hit, the nerds-with-technology anthem that both reflected and solidified his image as a gear-twisting studio shut-in. It matters not though, because we've all heard Dolby's many other compositions hundreds of times without even knowing Dolby had anything to do with them. As the founder of numerous computerized-audio companies, he's written and adapted hundreds of cell phone ringtones, including that ubiquitous Nokia factory-installed one. So he's a millionaire now.

FREAK NASTY, "Da' Dip" (#15 in 1997)

After his career stalled, Stephen Burnett (his real name is not Freak Nasty, unfortunately) became a high school teacher in Alameda, California. His musical past was an open secret and in 2004, he fulfilled years of student requests and performed the catchy, rapid-fire, minor dance craze-inspiring rap hit "Da' Dip" at the annual school talent school. He was reprimanded when, true to his name, he freaked an underage student backup dancer a little too nastily.

REDNEX, "Cotton Eye Joe" (#25 in 1995)

A series of studio musicians and singers, Rednex was assembled by Swedish record producers Janne Ericsson, Öban Öberg, and Pat Reiniz, who thought it would be a good idea to combine American hillbilly music with Euro dance pop. The band's debut was a thumping dance version of the nineteenth-century folk song "Cotton Eye Joe," which sold more than 10 million copies worldwide. In May 2007, Ericsson, Öberg, and Reiniz realized that the group had probably run its course and put Rednex AB—the corporation handling the band's business—for sale on eBay. The asking price: $1.5 million. The winning buyer would get the "band" and everything associated with it: trademarks, profits from future tours, and back catalog rights. There were no bids.

<< ▭ >>

One would think that a spot in a major rock band would be one to cling to tenaciously and with great vigor, but rock bands have a lot of turnover. It's quite literally a game of

Musical Chairs

THE 4 SINGERS OF VAN HALEN

Van Halen was formed in Pasadena in 1972 by brothers Alex and Eddie Van Halen, with Michael Anthony on bass and **DAVID LEE ROTH (SINGER #1)** on lead vocals. Discovered by Gene Simmons of KISS, the group went on to become the most popular hard rock band in the world in the 1980s. But in 1985, the charismatic but silly Roth frequently clashed with the charismatic but tyrannical Eddie Van Halen—Roth wanted to delay recording a follow-up to the band's landmark *1984* so that he could work on a solo album. As the band is named Van Halen, and not Roth, Roth got fired. His replacement: **SAMMY HAGAR (#2)**, the former lead singer of Montrose, and at the time a solo success with hits like "Three Lock Box" and "I Can't Drive 55." Despite repeated trips into sensitive, cheesy love ballad territory, and an overwhelmingly pro-Roth sentiment among hardcore fans, the band's tenure with Hagar was more commercially successful than it was with Roth.

In 1996, Hagar balked on making a greatest hits album, which Eddie Van Halen wanted to do. So, Van Halen went behind Hagar's back and hired David Lee Roth to sing on the customary and customarily subpar "two new tracks" that would appear on *The Best Of, Volume 1* that was now definitely happening because Hagar wasn't around to block it. Roth, elated to be back in the band after a decade of obscurity, happily recorded the unremarkable "Me Wise Magic" and "Can't Get This Stuff No More." Roth assumed he was back in the band for good. He wasn't. Behind the backs of both Hagar and Roth, Van Halen had recruited a new lead singer, a Los Angeles session vocalist named **MITCH MALLOY (#3)**. Malloy recorded some demos with the band, but he was never publicly announced as the new lead singer of Van Halen.

Then in September 1996, Van Halen made a surprise appearance presenting a trophy at the MTV Video Music

Awards . . . with Roth. With this very public stunt, as well as the newly recorded tracks, Roth firmly and reasonably believed he was back in the group, and was comfortable enough to mug and dance around for audience attention while Beck accepted an award. As he had 11 years earlier, Eddie Van Halen grew exasperated with Roth's antics and fired him again. Mitch Malloy, meanwhile, had no idea Roth had recorded songs with the band and didn't even know Roth was back in the band's orbit until he saw the VMAs on live TV. Feeling very rightfully dicked around, Malloy tendered his resignation. Having gone from nearly having simultaneously three lead singers unaware of each other, like some sort of *Three's Company* episode in which Jack Tripper has dates with three girls at the same time in the same restaurant and it all blows up in his face, Van Halen had now alienated and lost all three of its singers.

So, they hired former Extreme singer **GARY CHERONE (#4)**. His 1998 album with the band, *Van Halen III*, debuted at #1 and was a return to bombastic hard rock after the schmaltzy Hagar years, but it would prove to be Cherone's only album with the band . . . and Van Halen's last studio release to date. Cherone was gone by the end of the year. The band went without a singer until 2007, when it hired Roth back for a summer tour. Hard feelings were set aside; everybody needed the money. But it wasn't quite a reunion of the original lineup. Because he dared associate with Sammy Hagar in his off time, bassist (and the best harmonizing backup singer in rock history) Michael Anthony was kicked out of the band. He was replaced with 15-year-old Wolfgang Van Halen, son of Eddie, which at least increased the truthfulness of the band's awesome Nordic name to a solid 75 percent.

THE 8 SINGERS OF BLACK SABBATH

OZZY OSBOURNE (SINGER #1) was the lead vocalist from the time Black Sabbath emerged from Satan's loins in 1968, until 1977, when he left for a solo career. The band hired blues-era Fleetwood Mac singer **DAVE WALKER (#2)** to sit in, who performed with the band just once on a BBC show called *Look! Hear!* Osbourne returned in 1978, but by 1979 his drinking problem was so severe that the band fired him (because it made him unreliable; it's impossible to get fired from a metal band for being an alcoholic). Manager Don Arden's daughter Sharon (who later married Ozzy and gave birth to their loathsome children Jack and Kelly) suggested they hire the diminutive, powerfully voiced metal god **RONNIE JAMES DIO (#3)** of the band Rainbow.

In 1982, after a power struggle between Dio and the rest of the band (who accused the leprechaun-like Dio of mischievously sneaking into the studio to make his voice louder on finished tracks), Dio left to form his own band. Black Sabbath then used **IAN GILLAN (#4)**, one of Deep Purple's many former singers. The blues-oriented music he made bombed with fans, and in 1984 he left for a Deep Purple reunion. The band hired session vocalist **DAVE DONATO (#5)**, who rehearsed with the band but never performed or recorded with them. Osbourne returned to play a short but well-received set at Live Aid in July 1985. It was amicable, but Ozzy opted to continue with his lucrative solo career.

Sabbath filled Ozzy's dark and evil shoes with another former Deep Purple singer, the very un-metally named **GLENN HUGHES (#6)**. He got in a bar fight a few days before a 1986 tour was to begin, and he injured his neck and his vocal cords (proving he was pretty metal after all). For the tour only, he was replaced by an unknown New Jersey bar band singer named **RAY GILLEN (#7)**. **TONY MARTIN (#8)** of Alliance came on in 1987 and stayed for four years, until Dio returned for just a few months in 1991, and who was then replaced with Martin. Rob Halford of Judas Priest stood in for a couple of concert dates in November 1992, and so did Ozzy, but Martin remained Black Sabbath's official singer until Ozzy finally returned, for good, in 1997.

THE 9 RED HOT CHILI PEPPERS GUITARISTS

HILLEL SLOVAK (GUITARIST #1) left the group in 1984, barely a year after its inception, to focus on his other band, What Is This? He was replaced by **JACK SHERMAN (#2)**, who was tossed aside in 1985 when What Is This? didn't work out and Slovak wanted back in the band. In 1988, Slovak died of a drug overdose at age 26.

His replacement was **DEWAYNE "BLACKBYRD" MC-KNIGHT (#3)**, a former member of Parliament (the greatest funk band of all time, not the House of Commons), who, shockingly, didn't have good chemistry with the funky Peppers. McKnight was out after only a few months, replaced with the 18-year-old guitar prodigy **JOHN FRUSCIANTE (#4)**, who won the gig on an audition. It was with Frusciante that the band had massive commercial success with the 1991 album *Blood Sugar Sex Magik*. By 1992, heroin had completely taken over Frusciante's life and he quit the band—while on tour in Japan. The Chili Peppers quickly flew out a replacement to the next tour stop in Australia, former Circle Jerks bassist **ZANDER SCHLOSS (#5)**. Before Schloss played any live shows, the band decided instead to cancel the tour altogether in the wake of Frusciante's traumatic departure. Schloss was out, and the band returned to the United States, where it played Lollapalooza in the summer of 1992 with a new guitarist, **ARIK MARSHALL (#6)**. He never recorded any material with the band, but he mimed Frusciante's parts in the "Breaking the Girl" video and was fortunate enough to be part of the band when it was immortalized on the "Krusty Gets Kancelled" episode of *The Simpsons*.

After a series of open auditions in 1993 in which bassist Flea told *Rolling Stone* that they tested "thousands" of guitarists, they settled on a guy named **JESSE TOBIAS (#7)**. A few tense songwriting sessions were held, and when the band found that he had no chemistry with them, he was let go. Around the same time, Jane's Addiction, the *other* quintessential drug-addled L.A. alt-rock band, broke up. And so, Jane's Addiction guitarist **DAVE NAVARRO (#8)** became a Red Hot Chili Pepper. In interviews for their 1995 album *One Hot Minute*, Navarro humorously showed off to reporters the guitar picks he'd had specially made that listed his many, many predecessors. *One Hot Minute* was the only album Navarro made with the band. In 1999, Frusciante, drug-free, asked to be let back into the band. He lasted a decade this time, quitting again in December 2009. The band then announced that its new guitarist would be **JOSH KLINGHOFFER (#9)**, who was sort of an unofficial member of the band already, contributing to some Frusciante solo albums and playing with the band on its 2007 tour as an additional guitarist.

THE 11 (OFFICIAL) BEACH BOYS

And now, the most convoluted band history of all time. The original lineup, circa 1961, was: brothers **BRIAN WILSON (#1)**, **CARL WILSON (#2)**, **DENNIS WILSON (#3)**, their cousin **MIKE LOVE (#4)**, and their friend **AL JARDINE (#5)**. When Jardine stepped out to attend college in 1962, he was replaced by **DAVID MARKS (#6)**. A year later, Jardine reclaimed his spot.

In 1964, when Brian Wilson decided to be a studio-only member and not perform live with the group (due to mounting personal health problems), session musician and future variety show host/mugshot icon **GLEN CAMPBELL (#7)** was hired as his live-show-only replacement, contributing keyboards, bass, lead guitar, and some vocals. But after just a year, Campbell was out.

From 1965 to 1972, the band had a consistent roster of Love, Carl Wilson, Dennis Wilson, Al Jardine, Brian Wilson in the studio, and **BRUCE JOHNSTON (#8)** as his live stand-in. Johnston left in 1972 to pursue production, engineering, and songwriting work full-time. So the band made do with Love, the three Wilsons (Brian, increasingly unhinged, remained studio-only), and Jardine, with the addition of South African bassist/singer

BLONDIE CHAPLIN (#9) and drummer **RICKY FATAAR (#10)**, hired because their usual drummer, Dennis Wilson, got in an argument with his wife and punched a plate-glass window that so severely injured his hand that, for a couple of years, he was only able to sing and play keyboards a little.

In 1973, Chaplin left, then Dennis Wilson recovered, which made Fataar redundant. The Beach Boys reverted to its original five, with even Brian performing on stage, until 1978. He retreated inward again, and so Johnston came back. In 1983, Dennis Wilson left the band, subsequently drowned to death, and was replaced with **MIKE KOWALSKI (#11)**. Brian Wilson, a wreck inside and out, left the band completely in 1986, bailing before the Beach Boys' woeful county fair touring circuit era, experienced by Mike Love, Carl Wilson, Al Jardine, Bruce Johnston, and Mike Kowalski.

Brian Wilson rejoined in 1995 before leaving again in 1997. Carl Wilson would follow in 1998, owing to the conflict of his death from cancer. The Wilsons' two-for-one replacement: one-time early '60s temporary Beach Boy David Marks. He is still just considered a temp, as from 1999 to now, the only "official" Beach Boys are Mike Love and Bruce Johnston, making Love (who controls the band's affairs) the only original and continuous member. The touring support musicians are not given official member status, even drummer Mike Kowalski, who has been with the group since 1983. Other supporters include John Cowsill (of the Cowsills) and Christian Love, which is an admirable concept, a terrible name, and the son of Mike Love.

Many bands are named after the guy in the band who has all the charisma, writes all the songs, and sings all the songs, like Ben Folds Five or the Jimi Hendrix Experience. Confusing then are the

Bands and Solo Acts in Which the Titular Member or Named Person Is Not the Lead Singer

KOOL AND THE GANG

Robert "Kool" Bell is primarily the guitarist. J. T. Taylor was the band's singer during its late '70s and early '80s heyday on songs like "Joanna" and "Ladies' Night."

TED NUGENT

The guitarist for the Amboy Dukes and Damn Yankees was the highest-grossing live act as a solo performer in the United States in 1973. He sang lead on his biggest solo hit, "Cat Scratch Fever," but his other well-known (and better) song, "Stranglehold," was sung by the Nuge's longtime hired vocalist Derek St. Holmes.

MANFRED MANN'S EARTH BAND

Manfred Mann was the keyboardist. The singer on the band's only #1 hit, "Blinded by the Light," was a guy named Chris Thompson.

ELVIN BISHOP

Although Bishop occasionally sings, the song for which he is best known, 1976's "Fooled Around and Fell in Love" is sung by Mickey Thomas, the shrill-voiced banshee who would later front the abomination that was Starship.

SLASH'S SNAKEPIT

Eric Dover was the guitarist of the great power pop band Jellyfish and the lead singer of Slash's buy-us-for-my-name band comprised mostly of former Guns N' Roses members who look to Slash for any and all career decisions because they're too wasted to make any of their own. (See also Velvet Revolver.)

SERGIO MENDES

Mendes was famous in the 1960s for his bachelor pad/bossa nova instrumentals recorded as Sergio Mendes and Brasil '66 ("Mas Que Nada"), and again in the 1980s for peddling cheesy lite jazz/lite rock ("Never Gonna Let You Go"). Mendes, who served as a pianist and bandleader, didn't even credit a band in the '80s, only himself. The singer on "Never Gonna Let You Go," among others, was session singer and background musician Joe Pizzulo.

SANTANA

While Carlos Santana gained truckloads of filthy lucre and disgusting Grammys for staging a comeback in

1999 by latching on to popular pop and rock singers of the day, Rob Thomas and Wyclef Jean had to act like Santana was doing *them* the favor for "Smooth" and "Maria Maria," respectively. Santana was never a singer, because singing gets in the way of endless guitar noodling. Gregg Rolie sang lead on Santana's early classic hits, most notably "Evil Ways" and "Black Magic Woman." Then he formed Journey and let Steve Perry sing, because just try to stop Steve Perry from singing.

MIKE + THE MECHANICS

The band best known for the soft rock staple "All I Need Is a Miracle" and the Casey Kasem "Long Distance Dedication" standard "The Living Years" was both a side project and a supergroup. The "Mike" in Mike + the Mechanics is bassist Mike Rutherford, also the bassist and sometime guitarist in Genesis. Among the other Mechanics is singer Paul Carrack, formerly of Squeeze.

THE EDGAR WINTER GROUP

The albino guitar god does not sing; he can only shred. So guitarist Rick Derringer and guitarist/bassist Dan Hartman shared the band's vocal chores. Both Derringer and Hartman went on to successful solo careers with one memorable hit each ("Rock and Roll, Hoochie Koo" and "I Can Dream About You"), but on "Free Ride," the Edgar Winter Group's only memorable hit with vocals ("Frankenstein" was an instrumental), Hartman was the singer. Curiously, another member of the Edgar Winter Group was guitarist Ronnie Montrose, who went on to form the moderately successful '70s hard rock group Montrose. Montrose himself was not the singer in Montrose—vocals were handled by Sammy Hagar, who of course would later provide the vocals for Van Halen, the world's most famous and successful band ever named after members who weren't the lead singer.

Similarly, there are a few acts with names that are assumed or believed to be the name or nickname of the lead singer, when in fact they refer to the band as a whole.

- **SADE** is the band; Helen Folsade Adu is the charismatic lead singer.
- **BLONDIE** is the band; Debbie Harry is the singer, and in the group's early years, took to wearing shirts onstage that read "Blondie is a band."
- **PJ HARVEY** is the name of the group fronted by Polly Jean Harvey.
- Nobody in **HOOTIE AND THE BLOWFISH** was named or nicknamed "Hootie" or "Blowfish." The group was named for two close friends not in the band, one nicknamed Hootie and one nicknamed Blowfish.
- And, of course, there's **JETHRO TULL**. There was no individual in that group named Jethro Tull.

David St. Hubbins of Spinal Tap once said that "It's such a fine line between stupid and clever." Unlike St. Hubbins, there are some extremely smart rock musicians (they tend to be the ones who avoid drugs and can articulate a thought when Henry Rollins interviews them). So,

Here Is Some Smart Guys

Guitarist **TOM MORELLO** of Audioslave (and Rage Against the Machine) graduated with a degree in political science from Harvard. He also did it with honors and also while keeping up an unfailing habit of practicing the guitar for eight hours every single day.

Singer/songwriter/hobo **KRIS KRISTOFFERSON** has a master's degree in English literature from, of all places, the incredibly exclusive Oxford University, which he attended on a Rhodes Scholarship, one of the most prestigious awards in academia.

Boston's 1976 self-titled debut album is pretty much the demo that guitarist/producer **TOM SCHOLZ** made in his homemade basement studio. Helping to build the studio and record the songs was the master's in mechanical engineering he got from MIT.

In 1971, guitarist **BRIAN MAY** had to discontinue work on his PhD in astrophysics at the Imperial College of London in order to dedicate more time to his band,

Queen, where he remained busy for the next 30-odd years. In 2007, May finally completed his doctoral thesis, entitled "A Survey of Radial Velocities in the Zodiacal Dust Cloud."

Singer and guitarist **GREG GRAFFIN** is a founding member of Bad Religion, the definitive L.A. punk band. There has never been much money or job stability in telling society how fucked up it is, so Graffin crafted a second life within the society he so very much loathed: as a career academic. He doubled-majored at UCLA, earning undergraduate degrees in both anthropology and geology. Graffin went on to get a master's in geology from UCLA as well. He then got his doctorate—in zoology—from Cornell.

In addition to being the most popular band of all time, many claim that the Beatles are the best band of all time (scientists say that they're actually fourth-best, sandwiched right between the Smiths and the Thompson Twins). To be one of the four Beatles is to be a very rich, very famous, legend in your own time. A handful of people can make a claim on the status of being the unofficial "fifth Beatle." There are, in fact,

Six Fifth Beatles

While still kicking around dingy clubs in Hamburg, Germany, the Beatles served as the backing band for **TONY SHERIDAN**, another British act trying his luck in *der Fatherland.* Sheridan got a German record deal in 1961 and the Beatles tagged along as session musicians on his (West German) hit "My Bonnie," although the song was credited to "Tony Sheridan and the Beat Brothers." (It was not credited to the Beatles because that word sounds a lot like *peedles,* a German slang word for penis.) For being a mentor and getting the band (albeit under an assumed name) one of its first big breaks, Tony Sheridan was truly "the fifth Beatle."

When John Lennon formed a rock band in his late teens called the Quarrymen (which later became the Beatles, obviously), he let his friend **STUART SUTCLIFFE** join, on bass guitar. Why bass? Because *anyone* can play bass. Except Sutcliffe. He was not as serious a musician as Lennon or one of his other bandmates, George Harrison, and Sutcliffe quit the band in 1961, ostensibly to follow his promising painting career. The next year, Sutcliffe died of a brain hemorrhage. He didn't live long enough to witness Beatlemania, and had he done so, and after not being in the band anymore, he probably would have died from a massive brain hemorrhage. But because he was in the original incarnation of the band (and because he also devised the band's signature mop-top haircuts), Stuart Sutcliffe was truly "the fifth Beatle."

PETE BEST was the Beatles' first drummer, from 1960 to 1961. He was fired and replaced by Ringo Starr because the rest of the band (including noted non-musician Stuart Sutcliffe) didn't think Best was a very good drummer, his name notwithstanding. He was in the band briefly and wasn't good, and today the only person who seriously makes a case for Best as the fifth Beatle is Best himself, who calls himself that to promote his frequent concert appearances in small clubs in Britain and the United States. For seriously believing that he is the fifth Beatle, Pete Best is truly "the fifth Beatle."

GEORGE MARTIN contributed more to the Beatles' music than anybody else that wasn't an actual Beatle, and probably even more than Ringo. He produced nearly everything the Beatles ever did (except for *Let It Be*—a Phil Spector–led production that Paul McCartney hated and that majorly contributed to the band's breakup in 1970). When the band started including strings and horns in their songs, Martin wrote the string and horn arrangements. For that, Martin is credited with moving the Beatles' sound away from simple rock 'n' roll ("Love Me Do"—no simpler than that) into more experimental, groundbreaking territory (*Sgt. Pepper*, *Revolver*, "Yellow Submarine"). This makes George Martin truly "the fifth Beatle."

BRIAN EPSTEIN was the band's first manager and, as the job requires, its first champion. He discovered the band, secured them their first record contract, came up with the idea to dress them all in matching suits, convinced them to work with George Martin, and handled their business affairs, even throughout the overwhelming onslaught of worldwide Beatlemania. Epstein died in 1967, and in hindsight, Lennon believed that the Beatles began to fall apart at that point. For turning the Beatles into *the Beatles*, Epstein was truly "the fifth Beatle."

Pianist **BILLY PRESTON** met the Beatles in their Hamburg days and hooked up with the group again when Harrison asked him to play the piano parts he'd written for "Get Back" and "Let It Be." Lennon was so taken with Preston's work that he asked him to join the band permanently. (Paul McCartney nixed it.) Preston was the only person ever to receive individual credit on a Beatles song—"Get Back" is credited to The Beatles with Billy Preston. Preston continued to have a long professional relationship with George Harrison, even recording Harrison's "My Sweet Lord" before Harrison did. For contributing to the Beatles' remarkable late-period sound, and for even being considered nearly an equal, Billy Preston was truly, and in fact, almost was, "the fifth Beatle."

Oh, rock stars! You and your surprisingly humorous, ironic, self-deprecating behavior.

You're Incorrigible!

OH, QUEENS OF THE STONE AGE . . .

Josh Homme and his rotating band of tightly rocking stoners are frequently amusing. For example, on a 2005 *Saturday Night Live* performance, Queens of the Stone Age invited guest host Will Ferrell to play cowbell on their song "Little Sister," which he did fully in character as Gene Frenkle from the great "More Cowbell" sketch.

But in 2007, the group executed an act of hilarity and irony so exquisite it could only have begun as a dare. Little is known about how it went down, but I imagine it began in a band rehearsal. The Queens were playing their 2000 song "Feel Good Hit of the Summer," in which the lyrics consist solely of this phrase, repeated: "nicotine Valium Vicodin marijuana ecstasy and alcohol . . . c-c-c-c-c-cocaine." Then somebody joked how funny it would be if they performed the song in a rehab clinic for an audience of recovering junkies. Well, somebody arranged it, and in November 2007, Queens of the Stone Age signed up to play a six-song mini-concert in a Los Angeles rehab clinic. The first song played: "Feel Good Hit of the Summer." They reportedly didn't even make it two minutes before their instruments were unplugged and security was escorting them from the premises.

OH, SERGE . . .

Singer-songwriter Serge Gainsbourg was the definitive Frenchman, or at the very least, the definitive French stereotype. He was painfully ugly, he smoked and drank constantly, and he was a dirty old man (even when he was young, he looked old) who somehow persuaded insanely gorgeous French models and actresses like Brigitte Bardot and Catherine Deneuve to have sex with him. In spite of all this, or, really, because of all this, Gainsbourg was a national treasure and sex symbol in France. His best-known song is "Je t'aime . . . moi non plus," a love duet recorded in 1969 with his wife, model/actress Jane Birkin that begins with her breathily purring her lyrics and ends with her having an orgasm. Banned throughout Europe, it was a smash hit in France. In the United States, it peaked at, amusingly, #69.

But it's not even Gainsbourg's most controversial song. That would be "Lemon Incest," another love duet, which Gainsbourg recorded in 1984 with his 12-year-old daughter, Charlotte Gainsbourg. The end product is a bizarre, tongue-in-cheek, darkly comic paean to incest that comes off like a union of Natalie Cole's duet of "Unforgettable" with her dead father, and "Je t'aime . . . moi non plus." The lyrics to the song, of which the title is a play on the phrase "lemon zest," go roughly something like this (except in, you know, French): "Your kisses are very soft / I love you more than anyone else, Daddy." That's Charlotte's part. Serge's part: "The love that we shall never have together is beautiful, violent, pure, and intoxicating / my delicious child, my own flesh and blood." To add to the thickly stacked layers of irony and weirdness: Gainsbourg's original lyrics are set to the Chopin étude "Tristesse," commonly heard at weddings; and the music video depicts the singers laying in bed together—Serge has no shirt on, and his 12-year-old daughter wears just a T-shirt and panties.

OH, EVERCLEAR . . .

Everclear is not generally regarded as one of the more clever rock bands, but singer Art Alexakis, who in the band's heyday would not shut up about his shitty dad

("Father of Mine," "Wonderful"), was dedicated to being a decent father to his own kids. In late 1995, Alexakis treated his four-year-old daughter's Portland day care center to an acoustic set by Everclear. Some naughty lyrics had to be changed, of course, so the band's single "You Make Me Feel Like a Whore" became "You Make Me Feel Like I'm Four," which sounds pretty delightful.

OH, MAYNARD . . .

Maynard James Keenan of Tool and A Perfect Circle is the only heavy metal musician (for lack of a better classification) in the history of western civilization who knows funny. He's dabbled in stand-up comedy, used Bill Hicks as an opening act for Tool, and appeared a few times on the sketch comedy series *Mr. Show with Bob and David*. But the funniest moment in Keenan's career occurred in 1996. As Tool was repeatedly being asked to perform at the series of "Free Tibet" concerts popular at the time, he declined in favor of expressing his own ideas about what was the most urgent concern facing the world: He printed up "Free Frances Bean" T-shirts. (Frances Bean is, of course, the daughter of the late Kurt Cobain and the alive—at press time—Courtney Love.). Love lashed out in the press, labeling Keenan a "media whore." Keenan was ecstatic. "Isn't that great?" he told MTV News. "I have the distinction of being called a media whore by *Courtney Love*."

Most alternative rock groups of the 1990s and beyond are all somehow born out of the Pixies. To keep track, here's . . .

A Handy PIXIES-Related Alt-Rock Bands Flowchart

START

PIXIES were Frank Black, Joey Santiago, Kim Deal, and David Lovering.

In 1988, Kim Deal formed a side project called **THE BREEDERS**, along with bassist Josephine Wiggs and drummer Britt Walford, later replaced by Jim Macpherson.

Tanya Donelly went with the Breeders over her previous band, **THROWING MUSES**, which she founded with her stepsister, Kristin Hersh.

Tanya Donelly left the Breeders in 1991 to form **BELLY.** She was replaced by Kim Deal's twin sister, Kelley Deal.

During a hiatus from the Breeders, Kim Deal and Jim Macpherson formed a band called the **AMPS.**

Kelley Deal formed her own band, **THE KELLEY DEAL 6000.**

Jennifer Finch was once in a group called **SUGAR BABY DOLL**, with Kat Bjelland of **BABES IN TOYLAND** and Courtney Love of **HOLE.**

Another member of Belly was Gail Greenwood, formerly in **L7**, also home to Jennifer Finch.

David Lovering was a member of **CRACKER**, an offshoot of **CAMPER VAN BEETHOVEN.**

Tanya Donelly's solo albums have featured drumming by David Lovering of **PIXIES.**

Paz Lenchantin was in **A PERFECT CIRCLE** with James Iha, Maynard James Keenan, and Jeordie White.

Jeordie White was in the touring version of **NINE INCH NAILS**, and Maynard James Keenan is the frontman of **TOOL**.

Billy Corgan formed **ZWAN** with Jimmy Chamberlain and Paz Lenchantin.

PUSCIFER is a pseudonym Maynard James Keenan uses for solo work. Among those who have contributed to that group are Tim Commerford and Brad Wilk of **RAGE AGAINST THE MACHINE** and **AUDIOSLAVE**.

Melissa Auf der Maur was in **SMASHING PUMPKINS** with Billy Corgan, Jimmy Chamberlain, and James Iha.

The lead singer of Audioslave is Chris Cornell, formerly the frontman of **SOUNDGARDEN**.

HOLE also employed Jill Emery, Eric Erlandson, and Melissa Auf der Maur.

The lead guitarist of Soundgarden was Kim Thayil, who contributed to Dave Grohl's death metal band **PROBOT**.

David Bowie is the guiding spirit and the grandfather of alternative rock. Who was asked to perform onstage with Bowie for "Fashion" at Bowie's 50th birthday party concert at Madison Square Garden in 1997? Frank Black, of **PIXIES**.

Dave Grohl contributed guitar work to **DAVID BOWIE**'s album *Heathen*.

END

PIXIES

Succinct Information in Column Form

YOU KNOW, LISTS (AND ALSO CHARTS)

Presenting some thematically similar things, one placed after another in ascending, descending, or no particular order.

lists

7 SINGING DRUMMERS WHO SING WHILE THEY DRUM

1. Phil Collins of Genesis
2. Don Henley of Eagles
3. Ringo Starr of the Beatles
4. Karen Carpenter of Carpenters
5. Levon Helm of the Band
6. Micky Dolenz of the Monkees
7. Sheila E.

5 TEENY, TINY WIDDLE ROCK STARS

1. Prince: 5'2"
2. Angus Young of AC/DC: 5'2"

3. Malcolm Young of AC/DC: 5'3"
4. Glenn Danzig: 5'3"
5. Ronnie James Dio: 5'4"

9 HIT SONGS FROM 1987
(with Unnecessary Parentheses)

1. Cutting Crew, "(I Just) Died In Your Arms"
2. Whitney Houston, "I Wanna Dance with Somebody (Who Loves Me)"
3. Samantha Fox, "Touch Me (I Want Your Body)"
4. Samantha Fox, "Do Ya Do Ya (Wanna Please Me)?"
5. Aretha Franklin and George Michael, "I Knew You Were Waiting (For Me)"
6. Bill Medley and Jennifer Warnes, "(I've Had) The Time of My Life"
7. Pretty Poison, "Catch Me (I'm Falling)"
8. R.E.M., "It's the End of the World as We Know It (And I Feel Fine)"
9. Beastie Boys, "(You Gotta) Fight for Your Right (To Party!)"

15 DIMINUTIVE RAPPERS

Lil Wayne, Lil' Zane, (Lil') Romeo, Lil' Troy, Lil Scrappy, Lil Rob, Lil' Mo, Lil Mama, (Lil') Bow Wow, Lil' Flip, Lil Jon, Lil' Kim, Lil Boosie, Lil Eazy-E, Lil' Cease

8 ROCK STARS WHO MARRIED MODELS

1. Jack White, to Karen Elson
2. Rod Stewart, to Rachel Hunter
3. John Mellencamp, to Elaine Irwin
4. David Bowie, to Iman
5. Ric Ocasek, to Paulina Porizkova
6. Billy Joel, to Christie Brinkley
7. Todd Rundgren, to Bebe Buell
8. Royston Langdon of Spacehog, to Liv Tyler (Bebe Buell's daughter)

7 BIG FAT RAPPERS, AT THEIR HEAVIEST
(Estimated)

1, 2, 3. The Fat Boys (750 pounds, combined)
4. Big Punisher (700 pounds)
5. Heavy D (395 pounds)
6. The Notorious B.I.G. (350 pounds)
7. Fat Joe (290 pounds)

7 KNOWN OL' DIRTY BASTARD ALIASES

1. Dirt McGirt
2. Big Baby Jesus
3. Sweet Baby Jesus
4. Osirus
5. Dirt Dog
6. Joe Bananas
7. Peanut the Kidnapper

7 ATHLETES WHO WERE IN HAMMER'S "2 LEGIT 2 QUIT" VIDEO
(and How They Were Thereby Cursed)

1. Jose Canseco: steroid scandal
2. Isiah Thomas: managed the New York Knicks into the ground
3. Andre Rison: Left Eye of TLC burned down his house
4. Roger Clemens: steroid scandal; also had an affair with troubled country singer Mindy McCready that she says began when she was a teenager
5. Kirby Puckett: died of a stroke at age 45
6. Jerry Rice: lost to Drew Lachey of 98 Degrees on *Dancing with the Stars*
7. Chris Mullin: an injury prematurely ended his NBA career . . . a career in which he played for the Golden State Warriors

7 NERDIEST REAL NAMES OF RAPPERS

1. Reginald Noble (Redman)
2. Percy Miller (Master P)
3. Cornell Haynes (Nelly)
4. Artis Ivey (Coolio)
5. Melvin Barcliff (Magoo)
6. Carlton Ridenhour (Chuck D)
7. Will Smith

NUMBER OF STUDIO ALBUMS
MADE BY THE JACKSON FAMILY

68: Jermaine has put out 13, LaToya 11, the Jackson 5 made 10, Michael made 10, Janet has 10, the Jacksons had 6, Rebbie had 4, Jackie 2, Marlon 1, and Randy 1. The only one to have never released a record on his own: Tito.

7 LONGEST TOP 40 HITS
(As Far as Radio Edits Go, or the Lack Thereof)

1. Guns N' Roses, "November Rain" (8:57)
2. Meat Loaf, "Paradise by the Dashboard Light" (7:55)
3. Cashman and West, "American City Suite" (7:42)
4. Guns N' Roses, "Sympathy for the Devil" (7:36)
5. Dick Hyman, "The Minotaur" (7:24)
6. Richard Harris, "MacArthur Park" (7:20)
7. The Beatles, "Hey Jude" (7:11)

9 GROUPS WITH SELF-TITLED SONGS

1. Bad Company, "Bad Company"
2. Black Sabbath, "Black Sabbath"
3. Bad Religion, "Bad Religion"
4. Iron Maiden, "Iron Maiden"
5. Porno for Pyros, "Porno for Pyros"
6. Talk Talk, "Talk Talk"
7. Living in a Box, "Living in a Box"
8. Meat Puppets, "Meat Puppets"
9. Night Ranger, "Night Ranger"

ROCKY THEME SONGS
(in Descending Order of Quality)

1. Survivor, "Eye of the Tiger" (from *Rocky III*)
2. Bill Conti, "Gonna Fly Now" (from *Rocky*)
3. Survivor, "Burning Heart" (from *Rocky IV*)
4. Elton John, "Measure of a Man" (from *Rocky V*)
5. Three 6 Mafia, "It's a Fight" (from *Rocky Balboa*)
6. Frank Stallone, "Two Kinds of Love" (from *Rocky II*)

6 SONGS ABOUT JACKIN' IT THAT AREN'T "I TOUCH MYSELF"

1. Green Day, "Longview"
2. Gary Numan, "Every Day I Die"
3. Tori Amos, "Icicle"
4. Atlanta Rhythm Section, "Imaginary Lover"
5. Buzzcocks, "Orgasm Addict"
6. Prince, "Darling Nikki" (first verse only)

4 SONGS ABOUT DADS DYING AND 1 SONG ABOUT MOMS DYING

1. Mike + The Mechanics, "The Living Years" (Dad)
2. Sting, "All This Time" (Dad)
3. Green Day, "Wake Me Up When September Ends" (Dad)
4. U2, "Sometimes You Can't Make It On Your Own" (Dad)
5. Metallica, "Until It Sleeps" (Mom)

8 TV SHOWS MENTIONED IN
BLACK FLAG'S "TV PARTY"

1. *That's Incredible!*
2. *Hill Street Blues*
3. *Dallas*
4. *Fridays*
5. *Saturday Night Live*
6. *Monday Night Football*
7. *The Jeffersons*
8. *Vega$*

THE EVOLUTION OF A BAND NAME

1. Miami Latin Boys (1975–1977)
2. Singer Gloria Estefan joins the band, necessitating a gender-neutral name change to the Miami Sound Machine (1977–1987)
3. The addition of Estefan blows the band up, requiring a reflection in the band's name, hence Gloria Estefan and the Miami Sound Machine (1987–1989)
4. Estefan becomes such a big star that anybody who isn't her gets dropped from the band's name. It's all mostly the same musicians, but albums since 1989 are credited solely to Gloria Estefan.

4 MUSICIANS PHIL SPECTOR REPORTEDLY
PULLED A GUN ON

1. John Lennon
2. Leonard Cohen

3. Dee Dee Ramone
4. Ronnie Spector

5 LIVE RECORDINGS THAT MAYBE WEREN'T

1. **ELTON JOHN, "BENNIE AND THE JETS."** John thought the song sounded a little flat, and so in keeping with the idolizing-a-glam-rock-star theme of the tune, John had producers add in crowd noise so it sounded like a concert.

2. **CHEAP TRICK, *LIVE AT BUDOKHAN.*** Recordings of the bass guitar were messed up, so they had to be over-dubbed in the studio. Fully live or not, it's still the best Frampton-less live album ever made.

3. **JUDAS PRIEST, *UNLEASHED IN THE EAST.*** Rob Halford had the flu and a less than stellar voice when the album was recorded live in Japan in 1979, so his vocals were, at the very least, touched up in the studio. Some rumors claim his entire vocal performance was a studio creation. But *Unleashed in a Recording Booth* does not sound very metal.

4. **SLAYER, *LIVE UNDEAD.*** The album was reportedly played beginning to end in a studio . . . but about 50 fans were there to hear it, so by that measure it's technically a "live" record.

5. **KISS, *ALIVE.*** Rumors suggest they overdubbed or rere-corded many songs or parts of many songs, but Gene Simmons insists their label, Casablanca, didn't have the money for that at the time. A live album is by nature a cheap project and that's what *Alive* was, so says Gene Simmons, the world's most trustworthy demon.

THE ONLY 3 CHARTING SINGLES
RELEASED BY TAG TEAM
(the Titles of Which Lay Out Tag Team's Career Trajectory)

1. "Whoomp! There It Is" (1993)
2. "Addams Family (Whoomp!)" (1993)
3. "Whoomp! (There It Went)" (1995)

ALBUMS SAVED AND THOSE THROWN
AT THE ZOMBIES IN *SHAUN OF THE DEAD*

Prince, *Purple Rain*: saved

Prince, *Sign o' the Times*: saved

Prince, *Batman*: thrown

Dire Straits, *Brothers in Arms*: thrown

Stone Roses, *Second Coming*: saved

Sade, *Diamond Life*: thrown

6 ROCKIN' PEDOPHILES AND PERVS

1. **GARY GLITTER:** Imprisoned in Vietnam for molesting two prepubescent girls.
2. **R. KELLY:** Charged with—but ultimately acquitted of—videotaping himself having sex with (and urinating on) a 14-year-old girl. He also married the singer Aaliyah when she was 15 and he was 27.
3. **JERRY LEE LEWIS:** At the height of his fame in 1958, the 22-year-old Lewis married Myra Gale Brown, who was not only 13, but was also his cousin.
4. **BILL WYMAN:** At age 47, the Rolling Stones bassist began dating Mandy Smith, who was 13 at the time.

When she was 18, they married . . . and divorced two years later.

5. **JONATHAN KING:** A one-hit wonder in 1965 with "Everyone's Gone to the Moon," he's best known as a producer, record company executive, and the man who discovered Genesis. In 2001, he began a four-year prison sentence for having sex with at least six underage boys in the '80s.

6. **JOHN PHILLIPS:** Papa John of the Mamas and the Papas had a consensual sexual relationship with *One Day at a Time* actress Mackenzie Phillips, *his own daughter*, for more than 20 years.

16 GEOGRAPHICALLY NAMED BANDS AND THEIR ACTUAL PLACES OF ORIGIN

1. **BOSTON:** Boston, Massachusetts
2. **KANSAS:** Topeka, Kansas
3. **ALABAMA:** Fort Payne, Alabama
4. **CHICAGO:** Chicago, Illinois
5. **OHIO PLAYERS:** Dayton, Ohio
6. **OHIO EXPRESS:** Mansfield, Ohio
7. **AMERICA:** Founding members Gerry Beckley, Dewey Bunnell, and Dan Peek were all half-American: Their fathers all met their mothers while stationed for military service in Great Britain. Since the band came together there, this makes them British.
8. **TEXAS:** Glasgow, Scotland
9. **THE MANHATTANS:** Jersey City, New Jersey
10. **THE MANHATTAN TRANSFER:** New York City
11. **GEORGIA SATELLITES:** Atlanta, Georgia

12. **MC5:** Short for "Motor City 5," the band formed in the Detroit suburb of Lincoln Park, Michigan
13. **OF MONTREAL:** Athens, Georgia
14. **BLACK OAK ARKANSAS:** Black Oak, Arkansas
15. **EUROPE:** Upplands Väsby, Sweden
16. **NASHVILLE PUSSY:** Atlanta, Georgia

Chart geeks are a very special subset of music geeks. These are the kind of people who savor, collect, memorize and analyze data and trivia about the positions of songs on the various weekly, yearly, and all-time music charts, usually those found in *Billboard* magazine. Chart geeks are fussy, weird, and off-putting, not unlike record store clerks . . . if record store clerks talked about math as much as they talked about music. Step into this strange, sad world with some

Obsessive Chart Trivia

(based on stats from the *Billboard* 200 album chart).

JANET JACKSON'S *RHYTHM NATION 1814* **(1989)** produced a record seven top 5 singles: "Miss You Much," "Escapade," "Black Cat," "Love Will Never Do (Without You)" (all of which hit #1), "Come Back to Me" (#2), "Rhythm Nation" (#2), and "Alright" (#4).

MICHAEL JACKSON'S *THRILLER* **(1982)** was the first of two albums to produce a record seven top 10 singles: "Billie Jean" (#1), "Beat It" (#1), "The Girl is Mine" (#2), "Thriller" (#4), "Wanna Be Startin' Somethin'

(#5), "Human Nature" (#7), and "P.Y.T. (Pretty Young Thing)" (#10).

The second album to generate seven top 10 hits was **BRUCE SPRINGSTEEN'S *BORN IN THE U.S.A.* (1985)**: "Dancing in the Dark" (#2), "Glory Days" (#5), "I'm on Fire" (#6), "My Hometown" (#6), "Cover Me" (#7), "I'm Goin' Down" (#9), and "Born in the U.S.A." (#9).

ACT WITH THE MOST TOP 10 SINGLES: Madonna, with 38: "Borderline," "Lucky Star," "Like a Virgin," "Material Girl," "Crazy For You," "Angel," "Into the Groove," "Dress You Up," "Live To Tell," "Papa Don't Preach," "True Blue," "Open Your Heart," "La Isla Bonita," "Who's That Girl," "Causing a Commotion," "Like a Prayer," "Express Yourself," "Cherish," "Keep It Together," "Vogue," "Hanky Panky," "Justify My Love," "Rescue Me," "This Used to Be My Playground," "Erotica," "Deeper and Deeper," "I'll Remember," "Secret," "Take a Bow," "You'll See," "Don't Cry For Me Argentina," "Frozen," "Ray of Light," "Music," "Don't Tell Me," "Die Another Day," "Hung Up," and "4 Minutes." This list will be amended to 37 when I can finally prove that "Keep It Together" is not a song that ever actually existed.

ACT WITH THE MOST TOP 40 SINGLES: Elvis Presley, with 104.

ONE WEEK IN APRIL 1964, THIS IS WHAT THE *BILLBOARD* TOP 5 LOOKED LIKE:

1. The Beatles, "Can't Buy Me Love"
2. The Beatles, "Twist and Shout"

3. The Beatles, "She Loves You"
4. The Beatles, "I Want to Hold Your Hand"
5. The Beatles, "Please Please Me"

The songs that have spent **THE LONGEST TIME ON THE BILLBOARD HOT 100** are "I'm Yours" by Jason Mraz (76 long weeks in 2008–09), "How Do I Live" by LeAnn Rimes (69 longer weeks in 1997–98), "Foolish Games/ You Were Meant For Me" by Jewel (65 tedious weeks in 1997–98), "Before He Cheats" by Carrie Underwood (64 never-ending weeks in 2006–07), "You and Me" by Lifehouse (62 godforsaken weeks in 2005–06), "Macarena" by Los Del Rio (60 interminable weeks in 1996–97), "Smooth" by Santana featuring Rob Thomas (58 soul-killing weeks in 1999–2000), and "How to Save a Life" by the Fray (an additional 58 soul-killing weeks in 2006–07).

EXTREME ONE-HIT WONDERS—ARTISTS WHO APPEARED JUST ONCE ON THE HOT 100: Shawn Colvin ("Sunny Came Home," #7 in 1997); Gary Numan ("Cars," #9 in 1980); Moby ("South Side," #14 in 2001); Lou Reed ("Walk on the Wild Side," #16 in 1972); The Presidents of the United States of America ("Peaches," #29 in 1996); Morrissey ("The More You Ignore Me, The Closer I Get," #46 in 1994); The Replacements ("I'll Be You," #51 in 1989); Yoko Ono ("Walking on Thin Ice," #58 in 1981); Tool ("Schism," #67 in 2001); Pete Seeger ("Little Boxes," #70 in 1964); XTC ("The Mayor of Simpleton," #72 in 1989); and the Insane Clown Posse ("Santa's a Fat Bitch," #67 in 1998).

In the 1980s, six different songs called **"HOLD ME"** appeared on the Hot 100. In descending order of success, they were performed by: Fleetwood Mac (#4, 1982); Teddy Pendergrass (#46, 1984); Menudo (#62, 1985); Sheila E. (#68, 1987); Laura Branigan (#82, 1985); and Colin Hay (#99, 1987).

CREEDENCE CLEARWATER REVIVAL had five songs reach #2. Carpenters also had five #2 hits, but since they also had a few #1s, it seems fair if CCR gets to keep the record. All five of CCR's also-rans are classics: "Proud Mary," "Bad Moon Rising," "Green River," "Travelin' Band," and "Lookin' Out My Back Door."

THE VARYING SUCCESSES OF JAMES BOND MOVIE SONGS ON THE POP CHART

- Duran Duran, "A View to a Kill": #1 (1985)
- Paul McCartney and Wings, "Live and Let Die": #2 (1973)
- Carly Simon, "Nobody Does it Better" (from *The Spy Who Loved Me*): #2 (1977)
- Sheena Easton, "For Your Eyes Only": #4 (1981)
- Shirley Bassey, "Goldfinger": #8 (1965)
- Madonna, "Die Another Day": #8 (2002)
- Tom Jones, "Thunderball": #25 (1966)
- Rita Coolidge, "All Time High" (*Octopussy*): #36 (1983)
- Nancy Sinatra, "You Only Live Twice": #44 (1967)
- Shirley Bassey, "Diamonds are Forever": #57 (1972)
- Chris Cornell, "You Know My Name" (*Casino Royale*): #79 (2006)

Here is some more precise, nitpicky, obsessive chart trivia, specifically

Obsessive Chart Trivia About #1 Songs

MOST #1 HITS ON THE POP CHART: The Beatles, with 20. They were: "I Want To Hold Your Hand," "She Loves You," "Can't Buy Me Love," "Love Me Do," "A Hard Day's Night," "I Feel Fine," "Eight Days a Week," "Ticket to Ride," "Help!," "Yesterday," "We Can Work It Out," "Paperback Writer," "Penny Lane," "All You Need is Love," "Hello, Goodbye," "Hey Jude," "Get Back," "Come Together"/"Something," "Let It Be," and "The Long and Winding Road"/"For You Blue." (Second place: Mariah Carey, with 19.)

#1 HITS BY FORMER BEATLES: George Harrison was chronologically the first of the Fab Four to do it, but he ultimately had just three: "My Sweet Lord"/"Isn't It a Pity," "Give Me Love (Give Me Peace On Earth)," and "Got My Mind Set On You." Ringo Starr has had, shockingly (as in shockingly high), two: "Photograph" and "You're Sixteen." John Lennon had, shockingly (as in shockingly low), two: "Whatever Gets You Thru the Night" and "(Just Like) Starting Over," the latter posthumously. Paul McCartney, including his stint in Wings, has had nine: "Uncle Albert/Admiral Halsey," "My Love," "Band on the Run," "Listen to What the Man

Said," "Silly Love Songs," "With a Little Luck," "Coming Up (Live at Glasgow)," "Ebony and Ivory" (with Stevie Wonder), and "Say Say Say" (with Michael Jackson).

MOST #1 HITS OFF OF A SINGLE ALBUM: Michael Jackson's *Bad* produced five: "I Just Can't Stop Loving You," "Bad," "The Way You Make Me Feel," "Man in the Mirror," and "Dirty Diana."

BIGGEST LEAP TO #1: In 2009, Kelly Clarkson's "My Life Would Suck Without You" debuted at #97, owing to a late-in-the-week debut on digital music stores. The next week, when it had a full seven days worth of sales to account for, the song soared to #1—a jump of 96 points.

BIGGEST PLUNGE FROM #1: Billy Preston hit #1 with "Nothing from Nothing" in October 1974. America's collective love of the song was extremely short-lived—it dropped to #15 the following week. It was replaced at the top by "Then Came You" by Dionne Warwick and the Spinners. Once again, the public was extraordinarily fickle and that song tied Preston's record, also falling all the way down to #15.

THEY HAD ONE HIT, BUT THEY MADE IT COUNT: Artists who appeared on the *Billboard* Hot 100 exactly once, in which that song went to #1:

- The Elegants, "Little Star" (1958)
- Soeur Sourire, "Dominique" (1963)
- Zager and Evans, "In the Year 2525" (1969)

- M, "Pop Muzik," (1979)
- Jan Hammer, "*Miami Vice* Theme" (1985)
- Bobby McFerrin, "Don't Worry, Be Happy" (1988)
- Crazy Town, "Butterfly" (2001)
- Daniel Powter, "Bad Day" (2006). This was the #1 single of the year 2006—the only time an artist has appeared on the chart with exactly one song and then scored the year's biggest hit with it.

STREAK: Between 1978 and 1986—nine years running—Lionel Richie wrote a #1 single every year. They were "Three Times a Lady" (1978, performed by Richie's group, the Commodores), "Still" (1979, Commodores), "Lady" (1980, performed by Kenny Rogers), "Endless Love" (1981, a duet with Diana Ross), "Truly" (1982, solo), "All Night Long (All Night)" (1983, solo), "Hello" (1984, solo), "We Are the World" (1985, with USA For Africa), and "Say You, Say Me" (1986, solo). It may have kept going (maybe), but Richie dropped out of the public eye after an acrimonious divorce (his wife caught him cheating, then beat him up) and he didn't record again until 1992.

#1 SINGLES WITHOUT THE TITLE MENTIONED ANYWHERE IN THE LYRICS:

- Nelly featuring Kelly Rowland, "Dilemma"
- Ashanti, "Foolish"
- Mary J. Blige, "Family Affair"
- Coldplay, "Viva La Vida"
- Jay-Z featuring Alicia Keys, "Empire State of Mind"
- John Denver, "Annie's Song"
- Stevie Wonder, "Fingertips (Pt. 2)"

MOST #1 HITS ON BILLBOARD'S MAINSTREAM ROCK TRACKS CHART: Van Halen, with 13

MOST #1 HITS ON BILLBOARD'S MODERN ROCK TRACKS (ALTERNATIVE SONGS) CHART: Red Hot Chili Peppers, 11

MOST #1 HITS ON BILLBOARD'S R&B CHART: Stevie Wonder, 19

MOST #1 HITS ON BILLBOARD'S ADULT CONTEMPORARY CHART: Elton John, 16

Stevie Wonder's 1984 hit "Part-Time Lover" reached **#1 ON THE POP CHART, THE R&B CHART, THE DANCE CHART, AND THE ADULT CONTEMPORARY CHART**, the first (and so far only song) to reach the peak of those four charts.

LONGEST STAYS AT #1:

- **HOT 100:** "One Sweet Day" by Mariah Carey and Boyz II Men, and "I Gotta Feeling" by the Black Eyed Peas (tie)—16 weeks
- **MAINSTREAM ROCK:** "Loser" by 3 Doors Down—21 weeks
- **MODERN ROCK:** "The Pretender" by Foo Fighters—18 weeks
- **R&B:** "Be Without You" by Mary J. Blige—15 weeks
- **ADULT CONTEMPORARY:** "Drift Away" by Uncle Kracker—28 weeks

COCK ROCK: Since *Billboard*'s inception of the Mainstream Rock Tracks chart in 1981, only 13 songs by women have made it to #1. The achievers are not surprising: a couple of Stevie Nicks songs, a couple by the Pretenders, and one each from Joan Jett and the Blackhearts, Heart, Quarterflash, Scandal, Eurythmics, Pat Benatar, the Motels, and Christine McVie. The number is down to six if you don't count the female-fronted but mostly male Pretenders, Blackhearts, Heart, Quarterflash, Scandal, Eurythmics, and Motels. The last time a woman topped the rock chart: Alannah Myles with "Black Velvet" in 1990.

AFRICAN-AMERICAN ARTISTS WHO HAVE HAD A #1 HIT ON THE HOT COUNTRY SONGS CHART: Just two guys have done it: genre superstar Charlie Pride and former Hootie and the Blowfish lead singer Darius Rucker. However, Pride has had 29 country #1s, and Rucker has had three: "Don't Think I Don't Think About It," "It Won't Be Like This for Long," and "Alright." Still, that makes just two mega-successful country music artists who are black . . . three if you count Clint Black.

Still more nerdy music chart minutia, but there's more than just obsessive trivia about singles and singles charts to pore over and memorize; there's also

Obsessive Album Chart Trivia

(based on stats from the *Billboard* 200 album chart).

PERFORMER WITH THE MOST ALBUMS TO EVER CHART: Elvis Presley, with 111. Frank Sinatra is next with 83, then Johnny Mathis with 73. To be fair, a substantial number of the albums by all three singers are greatest hits albums and compilations.

MOST TOP 10 ALBUMS: The Rolling Stones, with 36 (23 studio, 13 live or compilation albums). Sinatra had 34 (28 studio, 6 compilations), and the Beatles had 30 (17 original albums, 13 collections).

MOST #1 ALBUMS: The Beatles, with 19. Second place: Jay-Z, with 11. Cumulatively, the Beatles have spent 132 weeks—about two years and seven months—at the #1 spot on the *Billboard 200* album chart.

MOST CONSECUTIVE #1 ALBUMS: The Beatles, again, with nine. They were: *Beatles '65* (1964), *Beatles VI* (1965), *Help!* (1965), *Rubber Soul* (1966), *Yesterday . . . and Today* (1966), *Revolver* (1966), *Sgt. Pepper's Lonely Hearts Club Band* (1967), *Magical Mystery Tour* (1967), and *The Beatles* ("The White Album") (1968). Breaking the streak was *Yellow Submarine*, which peaked at #2 in early 1969 and was kept out of the top spot by *The Beatles*.

FIRST ALBUM TO SELL A MILLION COPIES: Harry Belafonte's *Calypso* (1956)

ALBUM THAT SPENT THE MOST WEEKS AT #1: The *West Side Story* movie soundtrack spent 54 nonconsecutive weeks—that's more than a year—in the top spot over 1961 and 1962.

FIRST ALBUM TO DEBUT AT #1: It's routine now for major releases to debut at the top, but albums used to rise to #1 the way singles usually do. The first album to start at #1: Elton John's *Captain Fantastic and the Brown Dirt Cowboy* in May 1975. Second album to debut at #1: Elton John's *Rock of the Westies*, five months later.

BIGGEST LEAP TO #1: In April 1997, the Notorious B.I.G.'s *Life After Death* moved from #176 to #1. This was because a handful of stores jumped the gun and sold the very anticipated record (B.I.G. had recently been killed) before its official release date (but they still registered with the SoundScan sales tracking system).

BIGGEST PLUNGE FROM #1: *Light Grenades*, by the rap/ rock/jam/passé group Incubus debuted at #1 in November 2006, selling 165,000 copies. The next week, it dropped to an astounding #37. The previous record was a drop to #21 by Marilyn Manson's 2003 album *The Golden Age of the Grotesque*. Both acts in question were aging bands with small but devoted fan bases large enough to earn #1 debuts, but too small to sustain those big sales. In other words, exactly 165,000 people still loved Incubus by 2006.

ARTISTS WHOSE ALBUMS HELD THE #1 AND #2 CHART POSITIONS SIMULTANEOUSLY:

- 1961: *The Button-Down Mind Strikes Back* and *The Button-Down Mind* by Bob Newhart
- 1991: *Use Your Illusion II* and *Use Your Illusion I* by Guns N' Roses
- 2004: *Suit* and *Sweat* by Nelly

- Bruce Springsteen nearly did it in 1992. He released *Lucky Town* and *Human Touch* on the same day in March 1992. *Human Touch* debuted at #2, *Lucky Town* at #3. (The #1 album that week: Garth Brooks's blockbuster *Ropin' the Wind*.)

BIGGEST ONE-WEEK SALES: At the peak of the boy band fad, *NSYNC's *No Strings Attached* sold 2.4 million copies in its debut week in March 2000.

MIDDLING PEAK CHART POSITIONS OF SOME CLASSIC ALBUMS:

- The Clash, *London Calling*—#27
- Public Enemy, *It Takes a Nation of Millions to Hold Us Back*—#42
- Patti Smith, *Horses*—#47
- David Bowie, *The Rise and Fall of Ziggy Stardust and the Spiders from Mars*—#75
- The Velvet Underground and Nico, self-titled—#171

THE BESTSELLING ALBUMS OF ALL TIME IN THE UNITED STATES

These are rounded estimates, because actual exact sales figures are not available—the Recording Industry Association of America (RIAA), the music industry's trade association and royalty payment tracking organization, keeps those close to the chest. Also, prior to 1991, record stores just told *Billboard* how many copies of each album they sold each week. Now, stores use Sound-Scan, a point-of-purchase system that accurately counts how many units are sold. Despite this, the best reference info available for how many copies a particular album has sold is the RIAA's platinum certification records.

1. Michael Jackson, *Thriller* (30 million)
2. Eagles, *Their Greatest Hits 1971–1975* (29 million)
3. Led Zeppelin, *Led Zeppelin IV* (23 million)
4. AC/DC, *Back in Black* (22 million)
5. Shania Twain, *Come on Over* (20 million)
6. Fleetwood Mac, *Rumours* (19 million)
7. Boston, *Boston* (17 million)
8. *The Bodyguard* soundtrack (17 million)
9. Garth Brooks, *No Fences* (17 million)
10. Eagles, *Hotel California* (16.8 million)

THE BESTSELLING DOUBLE ALBUMS OF ALL TIME
(Not Including Compilations or Live Albums)

1. Pink Floyd, *The Wall* (11 million sets)
2. The Beatles, *The Beatles* ("The White Album") (9 million)
3. Led Zeppelin, *Physical Graffiti* (8 million)
4. *Saturday Night Fever* soundtrack (7 million)
5. Outkast, *Speakerboxx/The Love Below* (5 million)

What does it mean to be metal? It means being hard, tough, evil, and extreme at all times. What then is not metal?

The Most Metal Facts of Metal in the History of Metal

oddly enough.

1. Despite his affinities for leather vests, bloody skulls, and all that is dark and unholy, Glenn Danzig of the Misfits is a strict vegetarian and told a reporter in 2002 that his biggest vice is candy. 𝔐𝔢𝔱𝔞𝔩!

2. The first time Metallica unveiled its totally metal band logo was when they used it on their business cards. 𝔐𝔢𝔱𝔞𝔩!

3. According to old tour contracts, Pantera wouldn't perform if a certain object was not in their dressing room. And that object was a 12-pack of the sugar-free, grapefruit-flavored soda Fresca. 𝔐𝔢𝔱𝔞𝔩!

4. Gene Simmons of KISS claims to have slept with more than 5,000 women, but one of them was Liza Minnelli, whose career he also briefly managed. 𝔐𝔢𝔱𝔞𝔩!

5. Steve Plunkett, the lead singer of Autograph (the '80s American metal band who did "Turn Up the Radio," not the '80s Soviet metal band everybody patronizingly pretended to like when they played Live Aid), wrote and performed the theme song for *7th Heaven*, the TV family drama about a kindly minister. 𝔐𝔢𝔱𝔞𝔩!

6. Josh Freese, a drummer in bands such as the Vandals, A Perfect Circle, Nine Inch Nails, and *Chinese Democracy*-era Guns N' Roses, was a session drummer on *Breakout*, the 2008 release by Miley Cyrus. 𝔐𝔢𝔱𝔞𝔩!

7. Bon Scott was not only the lead singer of AC/DC, but he also played the recorder. 𝔐𝔢𝔱𝔞𝔩!

8. The 1989 KISS hit "Forever" was written by KISS singer Paul Stanley . . . and Michael Bolton. 𝔐𝔢𝔱𝔞𝔩!

9. In the lead-up to the 2008 U.S. presidential election, Blackie Lawless, the singer of W.A.S.P., best known

for songs like "Animal (Fuck Like a Beast)," "The Torture Never Stops," and "Kill Fuck Die," endorsed 73-year-old, ABBA-loving Republican senator John McCain. 𝕸𝖊𝖙𝖆𝖑!

10. The bestselling death metal album of all time in the United States is *The Dethalbum*, by Dethklok, the death metal parody band from the Adult Swim cartoon series *Metalocalypse*. The highest-charting death metal album of all time is Dethklok's *Dethalbum II*, debuting at #15. 𝕸𝖊𝖙𝖆𝖑!

11. Metallica drummer Lars Ulrich was a teenage tennis phenom. 𝕸𝖊𝖙𝖆𝖑!

12. Tommy Lee was introduced to his (now former) wife, Heather Locklear, by his accountant, whose brother was Locklear's dentist. 𝕸𝖊𝖙𝖆𝖑!

13. *The Osbournes* is a thing that happened. 𝕸𝖊𝖙𝖆𝖑!

<< ▭ >>

In this game of

guess which is which! For when you break down and cheat, the answers are on page 132.

CHARACTER FROM THE *MY LITTLE PONY* UNIVERSE OR PROGRESSIVE ROCK BAND?

1. Galaxy
2. Utopia
3. Mullmuzzler
4. North Star
5. Pallas
6. Ribbon

7. Beachcomber
8. Gryphon
9. Echolyn
10. Steamer
11. Sundance
12. Marillion
13. Hawkwind
14. Reeka
15. Watchtower
16. Isis
17. Draggle
18. Fizzy
19. Sky
20. Paradise
21. Rhapsody
22. Masquerade
23. Platypus
24. Mimic
25. Posey
26. Starcastle

ANCIENT CIVILIZATION
OR DOO-WOP GROUP?

1. The Mongols
2. The Paragons
3. The Del-Vikings
4. The Phoenicians
5. The Dravidians
6. The Dells
7. The Toltecs
8. The Marcels
9. The Scythians
10. The Imperials
11. The Visigoths
12. The Carthaginians
13. The Castelles
14. The Larks
15. The Hittites
16. The Skyliners
17. The Sumerians
18. The Cleftones
19. The Assyrians
20. The Crests
21. The Kushites
22. The Coasters

POP-METAL MUSICIAN
OR FICTIONAL VAMPIRE?

1. Whitfield Crane
2. Barnabas Collins
3. Edward Cullen

4. Sebastian Bach
5. Eric Martin
6. William Pratt
7. William Rose

CHRISTIAN BAND OR SCANDINAVIAN BLACK METAL BAND?

1. Living Sacrifice
2. Eternal Oath
3. Day of Fire
4. Theory in Practice
5. Immortal
6. Nathanael's Creed
7. Underoath
8. The Crown
9. Eucharist
10. Dyscyple
11. Old Man's Child
12. Anointed
13. Shining
14. Embraced
15. Seventh Day Slumber
16. Ever Stays Red
17. Dispatched
18. As I Lay Dying
19. At the Gates
20. Leviticus
21. Skyfire
22. Wrench

LITTLE GIRL OBJECT OF FANCY OR LITTLE GIRL OBJECT OF FANCY THAT IS ALSO THE TITLE OF A MARIAH CAREY ALBUM?

1. Rainbow
2. Unicorn
3. Charmbracelet
4. Princess
5. Butterfly
6. Daydream
7. Sparkles
8. Glitter

ANSWERS

My Little Pony *Character or Progressive Rock Band?*

Numbers 1, 4, 6, 7, 10, 11, 14, 17, 18, 20, 22, 24, and
25 are ponies and unicorns and such from the various
My Little Pony cartoon series, toy lines, movies, and
books.

Numbers 2, 3, 5, 8, 9, 12, 13, 15, 16, 19, 21, 23, and 26
are terrible bands your older brother adores.

Ancient Civilization or Doo-Wop Group?

Numbers 1, 4, 5, 7, 9, 11, 12, 15, 17, 19, and 21 have
come to kill your men and take your women.

Numbers 2, 3, 6, 8, 10, 13, 14, 16, 18, 20, and 22 have
come to snap their fingers and make your women
swoon.

Pop Metal Musician or Fictional Vampire?

1. Whitfield Crane was the lead singer of Ugly
   Kid Joe.
2. Barnabas Collins was the principal vampire on the
   cult soap opera *Dark Shadows.*
3. Edward Cullen is the dreamy, sparkly vampire from
   the Twilight books.
4. Sebastian Bach fronted Skid Row, Damnocracy,
   and, of course, Hep Alien.
5. Eric Martin was the lead singer of Mr. Big.
6. William Pratt was the birth name of Spike, from the
   Buffy the Vampire Slayer TV series.
7. William Rose was the given name of Axl Rose, of
   Guns N' Roses.

Christian Pop Group or Norwegian Death Metal Band?
Numbers 1, 3, 6, 7, 10, 12, 15, 16, 18, 20, 22: Praise
    Jesus!
Numbers 2, 4, 5, 8, 9, 11, 13, 14, 17, 19, 21: Hail Satan!

Little Girl Object of Fancy, or Little Girl Object of Fancy
That Is Also the Title of a Mariah Carey Album?
Mariah Carey has released *Rainbow*, *Charmbracelet*,
Butterfly, *Daydream*, and *Glitter*. She has not yet released
albums titled *Unicorn*, *Princess*, or *Sparkles*.

CHAPTER 5

Lapses in Judgment

AMUSING TALES OF FAILURE

"Hey guys, now that we've scored a massive hit with our totally original sound,

Let's Try Something Else

How about a concept album? Maybe we could switch musical genres completely? Or, how about we just disappear for years and people totally forget they liked us, and when we come back, we're not good anymore! Good meeting."

FLEETWOOD MAC, *Tusk* (1979)

Stakes were high for Fleetwood Mac after its self-titled 1975 album (the first since bringing Stevie Nicks and Lindsey Buckingham into the band) and *Rumours*, the 1977 classic that sold 13 million copies in its first two years (and eventually 19 million total).

All the songs on *Rumours* are about the band's well-documented myriad couples painfully and bitterly splitting up (for example, Buckingham wrote "Go Your Own

Way" to Nicks, Nicks wrote "Dreams" about Buckingham, and Christine McVie wrote "You Make Loving Fun" about the guy she was cheating on husband/bandmate John McVie with). And yet the band itself didn't break up, probably because *Rumours* had just sold 13 million copies.

Maybe the band members weren't talking to each other much, or maybe they knew it would be too hard to top a massively popular classic, but the Fleetwood Mac album after *Rumours* was *Tusk*, a double album that switches and back and forth between palatable ballads written and sung by Christine McVie or Stevie Nicks, and an angry, murky Buckingham track he (over) produced himself that tries and fails to evoke Buckingham's idol, Brian Wilson, most often attempted with the use of kazoos and ukuleles.

Though singles "Tusk" and "Sara" were top 10 hits, probably because they were about the nasty side of love and a Stevie Nicks private emotional crisis, respectively, both perennial Fleetwood Mac song topics, the album itself was a considerable flop. *Tusk* initially sold "only" a million copies. Drummer Mick Fleetwood claimed it was because a single radio station played the whole thing pre-release and *millions* of people tape-recorded the broadcast. A more likely scenario: that it cost twice as much as a single LP and also, that it was terrible.

FUN BONUS FACTY FACT: When I was about 17, I thought it was a pretty funny put-on to tell people that my dad was a part of the USC Trojan Marching Band that played on "Tusk." When I was about 17½, I realized that everyone hates *Tusk* and that telling this lie made me look like both a jackass *and* a moron.

GARTH BROOKS, *In the Life of Chris Gaines* (1999)

Garth Brooks had sold 90 million albums entirely within the 1990s, nearly matching Elvis Presley's lifelong total in less than a quarter of the time. But like those of us who don't listen to contemporary country music, Brooks was completely bored with contemporary country music by the end of the '90s and wanted to try something else. When Paramount Pictures approached him to play the lead role in a film called *The Lamb*, a drama about a deeply depressed, washed-up rock star named Chris Gaines, Brooks thought that starring in a movie might be the cure for his rich-guy boredom.

Brooks decided that the best way to prepare for his first major acting gig (apart from his appearance as an old French whore in the excellent *Saturday Night Live* sketch "Old French Whore") was to go Method, and get deep, deep inside the head of the fictional Chris Gaines. Screenwriter Jeb Stuart was still working on the script for *The Lamb*, so Brooks took it upon himself to develop an elaborate backstory for the character. To wit: Chris Gaines was the Australian son of an Olympic swimmer, had been a massive superstar in the 1980s with a pop-rock band called Crush, won the 1990 Album of the Year Grammy for his solo debut, had gotten into a horrible car accident in the mid-'90s, and was now attempting his comeback. (Also, according to Brooks, one of Chris Gaines's favorite musicians and biggest influences: Garth Brooks.) *The Lamb*, Brooks decided, would essentially be, to him at least, a Chris Gaines biopic in which Chris Gaines would play himself. And he would portray him as a brooding, tortured soul in a leather jacket, goatee, and Christian Siriano haircut, a look that eerily foreshadowed the rise of Derek Zoolander.

This was already mystifyingly far away from the raucous honky-tonk country of Brooks's first hit from a decade earlier, "Friends in Low Places," but it got even weirder when Brooks announced that his next album, to be released in September 1999, wouldn't be a country album or even a Garth Brooks album. Instead, it would be *In the Life of Chris Gaines*, a Chris Gaines "greatest hits" album of pop songs that Brooks would both record and promote in character.

In November 1999, Garth Brooks hosted *Saturday Night Live*. The musical guest that night: Chris Gaines, who performed his newest song, "Lost in You," from *In the Life of Chris Gaines*. NBC aired a Chris Gaines special that was part concert film, part mockumentary, with Brooks appearing as himself in it to make it abundantly clear that this weird soft rock guy that nobody had ever heard of that was making his big comeback, was, in fact, Brooks in the middle of what might have been a midlife crisis. (Case in point: in 1998, just before this whole mess, the 36-year-old Brooks unsuccessfully tried out for the San Diego Padres. The balding star also told a reporter that one of the things he liked best about playing Chris Gaines was that it allowed him to have hair again.)

Despite the staggeringly ambitious premise and promise of the situation, the music was bland and unmemorable. "Lost in You" did reach #5 on the pop chart, but Brooks's gigantic fan base of gigantic country music fans was confused and bewildered by the project. *Chris Gaines* sold two million copies in the end, ultimately the worst-selling album of Brooks's career. The failure of the album prompted backers to cancel *The Lamb* movie. The character of Chris Gaines was permanently retired, and Brooks returned to country music.

THE KILLERS, *Sam's Town* (2006)

Hot Fuss, the 2004 debut album by the Killers, was a triple-platinum smash, a throwback to synth pop and New Wave that was the most exciting thing to happen in alternative rock since grunge. It produced the perfect pop song "Mr. Brightside," among others, so anticipation for album #2 was high, as were expectations. Then Killers front man Brandon Flowers decided to make those expectations impossible to live up to. He told *Giant* magazine that *Sam's Town* would be "one of the best albums of the past 20 years," and told *Entertainment Weekly* that it would "keep rock 'n' roll afloat."

And at first, it looked like he might be right. The lead, pre-album-release single "When You Were Young" was a sweeping, catchy epic that effectively merged the Killers' electronic sound with the bombastic air of arena rock. It was the most-played song on alternative rock radio for two weeks and heavily whetted the public appetite for *Sam's Town*.

"When You Were Young" had gotten Killers fans all excited . . . for a paranoid and restless concept album about the hollowness of Las Vegas, the Killers' hometown. Even more perplexing was that the band had dropped the New Order/Cure influence for a half-baked

'80s Springsteen/*Joshua Tree* vibe. *Sam's Town* sold 1.2 million copies, about a third of the business of *Hot Fuss*.

The band's next release, 2008's *Day & Age*, rejected the creative legacy of *Hot Fuss* a little bit more. The quiet lead single "Human" made it into the lower end of the top 40, while the album itself just barely cleared 500,000 copies, or about half as much as *Sam's Town*. The worst part: It was *another* album about Las Vegas, suggesting that the Killers no longer wanted to be either the new New Order or the new U2, but instead the new Red Hot Chili Peppers, what with that band's pathological, self-destructive compulsion to deconstruct the "meaning" of its homeland of California.

MEAT LOAF, *Dead Ringer* (1981)

Meat Loaf does a very specific thing—hard rock show tunes—very well, but for that sound to really pop, he has had to rely on songwriter/producer Jim Steinman. And for the follow-up to his multimillion selling 1977 debut *Bat Out of Hell*, Meat Loaf knew not to mess with what works. *Renegade Angel* was going to be more of the same operatic, huge-voiced, epic rock, as conceived by Steinman. But in 1978, Meat Loaf lost his voice, as in he completely blew it out and was unsure if he'd ever be able to sing again. Steinman had already written the songs for *Renegade Angel* and had such personal attachment to them that he couldn't bear to abandon the project, so he renamed it *Bad for Good*, and recorded it himself, even though his voice is mediocre, or at least nowhere near as good as Meat Loaf's. And as

Bad for Good used most of the studio musicians from *Bat Out of Hell*, the end result sounded like Meat Loaf karaoke.

Meat Loaf, meanwhile, tried to stay relevant and financially solvent, which he didn't do a very good job at because he starred in a string of flop B movies, such as *Americathon* and *Roadie*. He didn't get his singing voice back until 1981, which was, unfortunately, when *Bad for Good* was finally released. He was ready to record, but Steinman was only willing or able to give him the songs that weren't good enough for *Bad for Good*.

Steinman at least threw a few new tracks together in a couple of months to round out *Dead Ringer*, Meat Loaf's first album in three years. But the singer's shtick had grown dated in the interim, and Americans had moved on to New Wave, Van Halen, and Christopher Cross. *Dead Ringer* peaked at #45 and sold less than half a million copies in the United States. One single, the pretty good "I'm Gonna Love Her for the Both of Us" charted at just #84. Meat Loaf kept making albums throughout the '80s, to almost no attention . . . in the United States at least; he remained phenomenally popular in England, where even *Dead Ringer* was a #1 smash. He wouldn't have another charting single in America until 1993 with the Steinman-led #1 surprise comeback hit "I'd Do Anything for Love (But I Won't Do That)."

PETER FRAMPTON, *I'm in You* (1977)

Peter Frampton was probably the biggest rock star in the world in 1976, coming off of the landmark *Frampton*

Comes Alive! album, which sold six million copies, remarkable because before its release, he was virtually unknown in the United States to all but the most hardcore fans of British blues-rock—Frampton had gotten his start in Humble Pie. Nevertheless, when it came time to release a follow-up to *Comes Alive!*, one would expect that Frampton would give the masses more of the same: hook-filled pop songs like "Baby I Love Your Way" and "Show Me the Way" embellished with guitar virtuoso tricks and that cool talking guitar robot voice thing. In fact, one might have expected it to be *nothing but* the cool talking guitar robot voice thing. That's not what happened. Frampton's *I'm in You* consisted almost completely of rock/funk fusion. But where Frampton really missed the mark is that there isn't much guitar work on the record.

Critics, who'd largely hated the pretty, poppy Frampton up to that point, liked the album because it was so undecidedly poppy, what with all the experimental synthesizer riffs and eight-minute funk odysseys. The title track went to #2, but the album itself sold about a million copies, which, for Peter Frampton in 1977, is basically nothing. Frampton attempted to get his career back on track in 1978 by what he thought was placating the mainstream, starring in the *Sgt. Pepper's Lonely Hearts Club Band* movie. Rightfully remembered as one of the worst movies of all time, the even worse soundtrack was mostly Frampton and the Bee Gees playing the beloved, not yet old songs of the Beatles. Frampton's career never actually did recover.

There's an old saying that goes something like, "Show me a beautiful woman and I will show you a man who has grown tired of sleeping with her." This is the sentiment at play when a musician leaves a band in the name of

Going Solo

PETER GABRIEL LEAVES GENESIS

When Gabriel was the lead singer of Genesis in the early '70s, it was a wild prog rock operation with lasers and shattering glass sound effects and cross-dressing and all other sorts of weird awesome stuff. Gabriel left the band in 1975, because he had a family, and because he was bored. Genesis auditioned new lead singers, many of them already incredibly famous, including Jeff Lynne of the Electric Light Orchestra, Phil Lynott of Thin Lizzy, Peter Frampton (who is also something of a guitarist), and even David Cassidy of the Partridge Family.

Genesis ultimately decided to let their drummer and backing vocalist, Phil Collins, take the job. The first Collins-led Genesis album *A Trick of the Tail* outsold all their Gabriel-fronted records combined because, like with Rod Stewart, the public just can't get enough Phil Collins for a reason scientists will never fully understand. Genesis rapidly turned into a top 40 band, and Gabriel's solo career has been a mixed bag; he pretty much does whatever he wants and his loyal fan base eats it up, be it impenetrable world music, or elegant understated pop like "Solsbury Hill." Gabriel has sold about

10 million albums in the United States, which, consider-ing his reluctance to do anything overtly commercial, is remarkable. The overtly commercial Genesis, however, has sold 20 million albums—twice as many as Gabriel—without Gabriel.

FERGIE AND WILL.I.AM LEAVE THE BLACK EYED PEAS

After years of obscurity with everyone but fans of alternative hip-hop (that is, white college students in the Northeast), the Black Eyed Peas reformulated its lineup in 2003, adding a scantily clad lady singer and rapper named Fergie. (Real name: Stacy Ferguson. She was part of the mid-1990s pop trio Wild Orchid and as a kid was a cast member of *Kids Incorporated*.) The theoretical eye candy (Fergie's appearance is a *touch* masculine) ploy instantly worked, and the Black Eyed Peas dived right into the mainstream, becoming both a tedious hit machine ("Where Is the Love?," "Don't Phunk with My Heart," "My Humps") and sellouts, appearing on every hackneyed network TV special (*Dick Clark's Rockin' Eve*) and commercial (Best Buy) offered to them.

In 2007, Fergie and Pea-mate will.i.am both decided to take a break from the band to work on solo projects. Fergie's was a wise decision. Her album, *The Dutchess* (Duchess . . . Sarah Ferguson . . . Stacy Ferguson . . . *get it?*) sold six million copies worldwide and spawned five top 5 hits in the United States, including three #1's: "London Bridge," "Glamorous," and "Big Girls Don't Cry." will.i.am (real name: William something) released his record, *Songs About Girls*, in September 2007. (It was technically his third solo LP, but the first since the Peas had grown popular.) It peaked at #38 and spawned three singles, with only one, "I Got It from My Mama," charting, but at a middling #31. *Songs About Girls* sold less than 100,000 copies in the United States, but it did go gold in Russia. Will.i.am's best-known solo work had been "Yes We Can," a YouTube video in which he set a hip-hop backing track to a Barack Obama campaign speech, and a remix of Bob Dylan's "Forever Young" for a Pepsi commercial, before he hitched himself to a hit machine that wasn't Fergie by contributing a guest spot to Usher's 2010 #1 hit "OMG."

ROBBIE WILLIAMS LEAVES TAKE THAT

Conventional opinion in the British music world was that if and when the immensely popular (in Britain) boy band Take That ever broke up, the member with the huge solo career (in Britain) would be the lead singer and dreamboat heartthrob Gary Barlow. Robbie Williams was a backup singer, filling the role of the rough-and-tumble, semi-rebellious looking dude that all the boy bands seemed to have (like that dude in sunglasses in the Backstreet Boys, or the dude with the goatee in the other one). Nevertheless, he left the group in early 1995 when he got tired of trite boy band music.

Williams's career has followed a trajectory similar to that of George Michael, late of Wham!: He left a pop group that did throwaway hits ("Back for Good") to make thoughtful, well-written, well-crafted pop songs ("Millennium," "Angels"). And Williams's first post-Take That recording: a cover of Michael's "Freedom!

'90." Williams proved the conventional wisdom wrong, going on to become one the bestselling solo artists in the history of the United Kingdom, scoring eight #1 albums and 27 top 10 singles, of which six went to #1. In the United Kingdom, Williams effectively became the next George Michael; in the United States, however, he's about as well known as Andrew Ridgley, the *other* guy from Wham!

THE KISS SOLO ALBUM GAMBIT

By 1977, KISS was one of the top recording and touring acts in the world—they had just earned a fourth platinum album award and were raking in about $10 million a year in concert grosses. The next phase: a publicity stunt in which all four members of KISS (Gene Simmons, Paul Stanley, Ace Frehley, and Peter Criss) would release solo albums simultaneously. Publicly, the band said it was to settle ego-driven disputes within the band, but in fact the idea was laid out in KISS's 1976 contract with Casablanca Records.

All four albums were marketed as KISS albums, with the title being the name of the performer (KISS: *Gene Simmons*, KISS: *Ace Frehley*, etc.). The cover art was also uniform, with an illustration of each performer in their KISS makeup. And they were all released on September 18, 1978, forcing your average teenage dirtbag KISS fan with eight bucks in his pocket to choose which one he wanted.

- **GENE SIMMONS:** Though the bassist in KISS, he did guitar work on his record, farming out the bass to a studio musician, suggesting that even bass players think playing the bass is boring. Also contributing were Rick Nielsen of Cheap Trick, Joe Perry of Aerosmith . . . and Helen Reddy. And Donna Summer. And Cher. Most perplexing is a straightforward cover of "When You Wish Upon a Star." It charted the highest of the solo discs, at #22.

- **PETER CRISS:** Being the singer of the surprise hit ballad "Beth," he stuck with that and did a lot of slow numbers (and the only instrument he played on anything was the drums, his usual instrument), along with a cover of Bobby Lewis's "Tossin' and Turnin'." It peaked at #43.

- **PAUL STANLEY:** It charted at a surprisingly low #40, considering that Stanley was KISS's front man and primary songwriter, and that unlike Simmons's and Criss's records, this was a hard rock album squarely in the vein of KISS.

- **ACE FREHLEY:** Simmons and Stanley were the biggest names in the group, but Ace's album sold the most (and it peaked at #26). His is also the only to spawn a hit: "New York Groove" reached #13.

The stunt didn't really work—four KISS albums all at once cannibalized sales. Of the five million copies total shipped of all four albums, only a million in all sold. The band pretended to patch up its make-believe problems and regrouped for 1979's *Dynasty*, which reached #9 on the album chart, went platinum in two months, and spawned the hit singles "I Was Made for Lovin' You" and "Sure Know Something."

THE GOING SOLO SCORECARD

GOOD IDEA; THEY WERE HOLDING YOU BACK: Paul Simon of Simon and Garfunkel, George Michael of Wham!, Justin Timberlake of *NSYNC, Bobby Brown of New Edition, Linda Ronstadt of the Stone Poneys, Smokey Robinson of the Miracles, R. Kelly of Public Announcement, Belinda Carlisle of the Go-Go's, Michael Jackson of the Jackson 5, Curtis Mayfield of the Impressions, Colin Hay of Men at Work, and John Fogerty of Creedence Clearwater Revival.

YOU LEFT THE BAND, TOOK A RADICAL LEFT TURN, AND BECAME COMPLETELY INTOLERABLE: Gwen Stefani of No Doubt, Lionel Richie of the Commodores, Roger Waters of Pink Floyd, Michael McDonald of the Doobie Brothers, Will Smith of DJ Jazzy Jeff and the Fresh Prince, Lindsey Buckingham of Fleetwood Mac, Sting of the Police, Susanna Hoffs of the Bangles, Peter Cetera of Chicago, Debbie Harry of Blondie, Natalie Merchant of 10,000 Maniacs, and Everlast of House of Pain.

And then there was the inventive, brainy Texas punk band At the Drive-In, who after a commercial breakthrough in 2000 with *Relationship of Command* and the hit single "One Armed Scissor," split up into two bands: the unremarkable emo band Sparta and the hostile-to-melody prog/metal outfit the Mars Volta.

GOOD WITH OR WITHOUT THE BAND: Stevie Nicks of Fleetwood Mac, Morrissey of the Smiths, Raphael Saadiq of Tony! Toni! Toné!, Annie Lennox of Eurythmics, Q-Tip of A Tribe Called Quest, Rob Zombie of White Zombie, everybody from N.W.A., Iggy Pop of the Stooges, and Björk of the Sugarcubes.

YOUR BAND SUCKED AND YOU STILL SUCK WITHOUT THEM: Rob Thomas of Matchbox Twenty, Nick Lachey of 98 Degrees, Uncle Kracker of the Kid Rock entourage, every Eagle, and Vince Gill, who became a country superstar after leaving the now largely forgotten country-rock group Pure Prairie League (they did "Let Me Love You Tonight").

It's pretty amazing that of all the millions and millions of songs that have been written, there isn't more overlap of content. Of course, there is overlap, and sometimes it's a bit more than unintentional, as in it's absolutely intentional. In other words,

They Didn't Mean to Steal That Song (Except That Maybe They Did)

"I WANT A NEW DRUG" VS. "GHOSTBUSTERS"

HUEY LEWIS was a big deal in 1984, so the producers of the upcoming surefire blockbuster *Ghostbusters* asked Lewis—and his loyal band of merry men, the News—to write the movie's theme song. Lewis declined, and ultimately recorded the theme song ("The Power of Love") for the other great sci-fi comedy of the '80s, *Back to the Future*. So the *Ghostbusters* producers hired Ray Parker

Jr., the front man of Raydio, somewhat popular for a handful of top 10 hits that are now long forgotten. That was not the case with the song Parker made for the film. Inspired by the scene in *Ghostbusters* where the Ghostbusters make a Ghostbusters commercial, Parker came up with a song that sounds like a commercial jingle for the Ghostbusters called "Ghostbusters." The song ("Ghostbusters") hit #1 and the movie (*Ghostbusters*) made $292 million at the box office.

However, the movie scene might not have been Parker's real inspiration. Lewis sued Parker in late 1984 because the melody of "Ghostbusters" was very similar to the melody of his 1984 top 10 hit "I Want a New Drug." (It's really *quite* a coincidence how Lewis declined the opportunity to write the *Ghostbusters* song, how the producers of the movie found someone else, and how the replacement's song sounded *just like* Huey Lewis's.) During the course of the lawsuit, Lewis's attorneys discovered a letter sent to Parker by the film production advising him to specifically write a song similar to "I Want a New Drug," which is a pretty damning detail in a copyright infringement suit.

The case was finally settled in 1995; Parker was held liable for what he did and paid an undisclosed sum out the ass to Lewis, but other details of the case remained sealed with a legally binding gag order. Nevertheless, on his *Behind the Music* episode in 2001, Lewis dared to talk about the case. "It was kind of symbolic of an industry that wants something—they wanted our wave, and they wanted to buy it," Lewis said. A few weeks later, Parker once again copied Huey Lewis: He sued, for violating the confidentiality clause. *That* suit has probably been settled out of court by now, but since gag orders, and the violating of gag orders, was such a major part of this story, we'll probably never know exactly how much money, if any, changed hands, and if anybody does speak up, they'll probably get sued. Again.

"I WANNA BE YOUR BOYFRIEND" VS. "GIRLFRIEND"

In spring 2007, Canadian pop starlet **AVRIL LAVIGNE** went to #1 with one of the most annoying songs in recent memory, "Girlfriend." It begins with Lavigne chanting, cheerleader-style, about how she should be your girlfriend. The song sounded very familiar to Tommy Dunbar, lead singer and chief songwriter of the 1970s power pop band the Rubinoos, because he wrote part of it: The opening chant of "Girlfriend," Dunbar believed, bore a striking similarity to the chorus of his 1979 Rubinoos song "I Wanna Be Your Boyfriend."

Dunbar and his cowriter James Gangwer sued Lavigne, her cowriter "Dr. Luke," and her publishing company for infringement. Dunbar and Gangwer had no intention of making the case a public mess, but two days after the suit was filed, Lavigne's manager Terry McBride lashed out against the Rubinoos in the press, and thus brought it to the press's attention. In a shortsighted, potentially damaging move, McBride said the songs bore no similarities, and if "Girlfriend" was similar to any song, it was the Rolling Stones' "Get Off of My Cloud." So as far as McBride was concerned, they didn't have to give any money or credit to Dunbar, because his client stole from *another*, and far better known, song.

Lavigne took to her website to question the legitimacy of the suit. "I had never heard this song in my life and their claim is based on five words," Lavigne wrote, in regards to the Rubinoos song. "All songs share similar lyrics and emotions. As humans we speak one language." So, according to Lavigne, she may steal someone else's work—which she and her manager more or less admitted to—because it's all in the name of expressing the human condition. "I don't have to prove anything to anyone," Lavigne continued. Except that she apparently did have to prove something to someone, and didn't prove it very well, because in January 2008 the case was settled, out of court, for an undisclosed sum.

"THE LAST TIME" VS. "BITTER SWEET SYMPHONY"

In 1997, the Britpop band **THE VERVE** was recording its third album *Urban Hymns*, with the centerpiece being "Bitter Sweet Symphony." The song is built around a hook repeated throughout, a sample of the Rolling Stones' early hit "The Last Time" as performed by the Andrew Oldham Orchestra in 1966 (Oldham was the Stones' first manager).

The Verve negotiated a license to use the sample of the orchestral "The Last Time" via the owner of the song's copyright, ABKCO Publishing. Both sides agreed to a 50/50 royalty split. The Verve recorded the song and released it as the first single off *Urban Hymns*. Upon hearing the song—and seeing that it was quickly turning into one of the most popular and critically adored rock hits of the year—ABKCO had second thoughts. Too late? Nope. ABKCO informed the Verve that their 50/50 agreement was suddenly null and void because "Bitter Sweet Symphony" relied too heavily on the sample of "The Last Time." (And honestly, it does—it's pretty much just lead singer Richard Ashcroft singing his lyrics over the forever-repeating looped sample.) Instead, ABKCO demanded, or some may say extorted, 100 percent of the royalties for the song, or it would have the album removed from store shelves. Not wanting their entire album banned forever, the Verve relented.

And so, the copyright of "Bitter Sweet Symphony" came under the control of ABKCO, who has since earned 100 percent of the royalties from it. Because one dick move deserves another, ABKCO even revised the tune's songwriting credit to "Jagger/Richards," despite Ashcroft writing lyrics. And since ABKCO owns the song, the company has used it in commercials for Nike and Vauxhall cars. Ashcroft finds it all quite appalling. "Don't buy Vauxhall cars," Ashcroft told a concert audience shortly after one ad ran. "They're shite cars."

<< ▭ >>

Disco made cocaine a billion-dollar industry and home ownership a reality for countless studio violinists. It was such an all-encompassing fad that many musicians felt that they had to embrace it or risk oblivion. Here are some artists who maybe should have chosen oblivion instead of

Going Disco

FRANK SINATRA

"Night and Day" is one of the most famous standards in music history. It was written by Cole Porter and first sung in 1932 in the musical *Gay Divorce* by Fred Astaire, but in the 1950s, Frank Sinatra turned it into one of his many signature songs. You would think that in the late '70s when some guy proposed to him a disco record, Sinatra would've dismissed this new crazy, kooky musical fad as ring-a-ding, 18-karat bombsville baby, and have a trusted Sicilian "business associate" kill the punk who asked him to do it execution-style, but in 1977, Sinatra actually recorded a disco version of "Night and Day." It was released as a stand-alone, non-album single, and was an obvious, pride-swallowing, and embarrassing ploy for some disco cash. It didn't work, probably because Sinatra fans were old and definitely not into disco, while disco fans were young and definitely not into Sinatra. The new "Night and Day" failed to reach any song chart.

ETHEL MERMAN

Apparently in 1979, some studio executive thought nobody was riper for a comeback, or more appropriate for disco, than mid-century Broadway icon Ethel Mermen. Her loud, brassy voice was suited specifically to belt out showstopping musical numbers like "Rose's Turn" from *Gypsy*, not breathy, sexy disco. No matter. Merman personally hated disco but really needed the money, so she agreed to the album. Rather than record new songs, she quickly rerecorded her old Broadway favorites, like "Everything's Coming Up Roses" and "There's No Business Like Show Business" while producers just sped them up and threw some generic pumping synth drums over them to create the cleverly titled *The Ethel Merman Disco Album*. It was released to little notice and sold poorly, but it's something of a camp classic for fans of the musical theater.

KISS

Disco was a potentially lucrative fad, and KISS is always there to cash in on any profit-making opportunity, be it comic books, action figures, or even disco, the philosophical opposite of KISS in the '70s. Nevertheless, "I Was Made for Lovin' You" was an experiment in KISS disco and was the first single the band released after its disappointing attempt in 1978 to release solo albums by all four members (see page 146). It's actually one of KISS's better songs—not terribly surprising, as good disco has catchy, thumping bass lines, and KISS's music has catchy, thumping bass lines—and one of their biggest hits, reaching #11 in 1979, second only to the ballad "Beth," another non-KISS sounding KISS song.

GRATEFUL DEAD

Of all bands, the Grateful Dead should probably stick to their shtick: endless, mindless instrumental noodling that you can dance poorly to because you're too high on an unidentified substance you smoked out of an apple. This is especially true of the 1978 album *Shakedown*

Street. Amid Jerry Garcia's painful and soulless attempts at funk and covers of "Stagger Lee" and "Good Lovin'" is the title track, "Shakedown Street," in which the Dead does disco. Philosophical and aesthetic similarities to disco aside (songs that last forever, it being better with cocaine), it's tedious and unbearable . . . even for a jam band.

BRYAN ADAMS

Bryan Adams has never been critically acclaimed, but he has provided plenty of agreeable straight-up rock 'n' roll. (He's like the Canadian John Mellencamp, who in turn is the poor man's Bruce Springsteen.) Adams's guitar rock has always been so fleshed-out and polished that it's hard to believe that his first single was a label- and studio-botched disco misstep.

In 1977, Adams and Jim Vallance, who would become his longtime songwriting partner, composed and recorded a mid-tempo pop song called "Let Me Take You Dancing." A&M Records agreed to release it in 1979, but thought that for the song to be a hit in the United States, where all the money was, it needed to be a disco song, the hot ticket at the time (except not really—the fad was dying by that point). So, A&M hired producer John Luongo to remix the song. In 1979 though, remixing a song into a disco track involved little more than just speeding it up and throwing on a thumping beat. So that's what Luongo did. But speeding up the music also meant that Adams's voice was sped up to the point of ridiculousness. The otherwise raspy Adams ended up sounding like an effeminate teen idol mid-voice change. The half-assed production, the disco beat, the indeterminate gender of the vocalist—it's like a lost Leif Garrett demo.

A&M was completely wrong about "Let Me Take You Dancing." In Adams's native Canada, the song made it only as far as #57 on the pop chart. It was a commercial failure everywhere else in the world, including the big American market. Nevertheless, A&M signed Adams to a long-term deal, and he settled into a successful rock career.

THE BEACH BOYS

Bruce Johnston joined the Beach Boys in 1965, but he continued to work as a songwriter and arranger for other artists. He worked on landmark recordings like Elton John's *Goodbye Yellow Brick Road* and Pink Floyd's *The Wall*. And yet, despite this pedigree and demonstrable good taste, in 1977 Johnston recorded a six-minute, disco version of "Pipeline," the instrumental surf rock classic by the Chantays. In full-on tacky disco fashion, the iconic guitar riff of the original is played by a group of violins in unison on the disco remake.

But as bad as Johnston's "Pipeline" is, there's a worse Beach Boys disco song. The band was flailing by the late '70s, far from their popular and visionary heights of the 1960s, and so in 1979 came a stab at regaining commercial relevance: "Here Comes the Night," an 11-minute disco remake of a song written and sung by Brian Wilson and Mike Love for 1967's *Wild Honey*. This version, however, featured vocals by the Beach Boys' JV squad: Al Jardine and Carl Wilson. It is, to

date, the only Beach Boys song to feature vocoders, the
Auto-Tune of the '70s.

"So hey, thanks for coming out to the show tonight. We
appreciate your support, and Steve's girlfriend Melissa is
over there at

The Merch Table

with some awesome T-shirts and our CD and some other
crap with our logo on it."

JIMMY BUFFETT may give the impression that he spends
his days and nights drunk off his ass on brightly colored
drinks at an undisclosed island location, but he's stayed
away from the margaritas long enough to develop a ton
of "Margaritaville" merchandise (or at least long enough
to sign release forms faxed down by his lawyer and business manager). Among the ways you can experience the
island flavor of Buffett's only hit: Dine at Margaritaville,
a Red Lobster-ish restaurant chain; eat Margaritaville-
brand frozen shrimp and chicken wings; wear Margaritaville-brand flip-flops; or make your own margaritas with
the Margaritaville Frozen Concoction Maker (just add
Margaritaville-brand tequila and Margaritaville-brand
margarita mix).

A casual **DANZIG** fan would buy and wear a black Danzig
T-shirt or put a black Danzig sticker on the back of their
AMC Pacer. A real Danzig fan buys the 80-page, college-
ruled, officially licensed Danzig spiral notebook, which

holds totally metal Algebra II notes securely inside with its black front and back covers, both decorated with the band's goat-skull emblem.

After kicking his addictions to alcohol and various drugs, Megadeth's **DAVE MUSTAINE** got heavily into gourmet coffee, ultimately releasing his own coffee line. Since Mustaine was once kicked out of Metallica, did the coffee consist solely of beans not good enough for Metallica Coffee? Perhaps, if such a thing existed. But the stuff was available at Megadeth concerts and on the band's website before Mustaine discontinued the line in 2009.

When shopping for your pregnant hipster girlfriend at **HOT TOPIC**, remember that while a black-and-white-striped "Johnny Cash Folsom Prison 1968" baby onesie is cool, the Guns N' Roses "Sweet Child O' Mine" baby onesie is way cooler.

We wouldn't know to have safe sex if it weren't for musicians in the '80s and '90s constantly telling us to do so (mostly George Michael and Salt-N-Pepa), but some artists actually went so far as to make **CONDOMS** with their names on them. So when you were about to get "down" (which is what they said at the time), you could choose between a safe, laboratory-scrutinized, pharmacy-sanctioned prophylactic, or a U2 Zoo TV condom, or a Frankie Goes to Hollywood condom, wherein if things are about to finish prematurely, you should just, you know, relax.

The undisputed industry leader in officially licensed garbage is **KISS**. While at this point even non–music geeks know about the KISS coffin (for example, Drew's dad was buried in one on an episode of *The Drew Carey Show*), Gene Simmons has allowed hundreds if not thousands of products to bear the KISS name, logo, or band photo. A full count is actually impossible. Seriously—there's even an electric toothbrush that plays a two-minute clip of "Rock and Roll All Nite," so you know exactly how long to brush. (Dental hygiene is way metal.) But while a coffin makes sense for a hard rock band with a horror bent, a coffeehouse in a tourist trap of a beach town does not. It's not technically a piece of merchandise, but the KISS Coffeehouse in Myrtle Beach, South Carolina, is something that really exists. The store has a job application online that includes a section on "I Rock Because . . . ," to which the best answer is "my commitment to customer service is totally rock 'n' roll." The Coffeehouse menu is typical coffee-house fare, although most items are given awkward KISS- or rock-themed names, such as the Demon Dark Roast blend, KISS Unplugged (decaf coffee), or the Karamel Rockiato. Assorted teas and milk are also avail-able, as are exciting franchising opportunities.

In 1994, **TOOL** had emerged as one of the hottest new bands in the country. The band's label, Zoo Entertain-ment, was contractually obligated to clear any merchan-dise or promotional ideas with the band before following through with production, but without the band's con-sent, they made a gross of child- and toddler-sized T-shirts emblazoned with the band's name, its penis-like wrench logo, and the name of its new single. Evidently, Zoo got the idea from Nirvana, which had made kiddie-sized T-shirts that proved popular as radio station give-away items. The problem is that the single the shirts were supposed to promote was "Prison Sex," a sexually explicit song about front man Maynard James Keenan's childhood sexual abuse. Despite that, and the song's non-ambiguous title, Keenan had to actually personally tell the label to not release the kids' shirts because the song is, as he told MTV News, "about getting fucked in the ass as a little kid."

Is the Grammy for Best New Artist Cursed?

Not really. It's not necessarily true that careers promptly die for whoever wins the award. It's more that the National Academy of Recording Arts and Sciences just happens to routinely honor undeserving acts.

1964: The winner was the Swingle Singers, a novelty act that set Bach compositions to jazz and scat rhythms, and then performed them a capella. Seriously. The group never achieved commercial success anywhere, but still records and performs to this day for audiences who like this sort of thing, which is like those smarmy a capella groups you avoided in college, except that the singers are extremely old. (The group beat out the now far more famous pop singer Vikki Carr and folk singer Trini Lopez.)

1979: A Taste of Honey beat both the Cars and Elvis Costello. Even other nominee Toto was more deserving than the group that did "Boogie Oogie Oogie" and then broke up less than three years later.

1981: For the first and only time, a single performer swept the top four awards. Christopher Cross won Record of the Year ("Sailing"), Song of the Year ("Sailing"), Album of the Year (*Christopher Cross*), and Best New Artist . . . over the Pretenders, one of the preeminent bands of the '80s and an inductee into the Rock and Roll Hall of Fame. Cross disappeared from public consciousness by 1985.

1990: Milli Vanilli was named Best New Artist, a no-brainer for the Academy because of the group's three consecutive #1 hits. But after it surfaced that the duo were lip-synching frauds, the award was revoked. It was not re-awarded to any of the other nominees: Neneh Cherry, the Indigo Girls, Soul II Soul, and Tone Lōc. While the Indigo Girls have a loyal following and have scored a couple of minor hits ("Closer to Fine" and "Shame on You"), I'd argue that the act with the most memorable songs is probably Milli Vanilli.

1992: Marc Cohn won on the strength of his remarkable single "Walking in Memphis." Since then, he's had no hit singles and four low-selling albums, but he did make the news in 2005 when he was shot in the head in an attempted carjacking in Denver. Not only did he live, he was hospitalized for less than a day. The piano-playing, delicate-voiced Marc Cohn, it would seem, is an unkillable badass.

1996: Hootie and the Blowfish sold about 14 million copies of its debut album *Cracked Rear View* in 1995, but America got tired of them really fast. Already a punch line by early 1996, the band still defeated long-term stars Brandy, Alanis Morissette, and Shania Twain for Best New Artist. Hootie and the Blowfish released two more good-selling albums in the 1990s and two poor-selling albums in the 2000s before front man Darius Rucker left for a quite successful solo career in country music.

1999: Despite having already established herself as a member of the Fugees, who in 1996 released *The Score*, which at one point was the bestselling hip-hop album of all time, the not new at all Lauryn Hill won the Best New Artist award. A listen to *The Miseducation of Lauryn Hill* (the year's Album of the Year recipient) proves she was a deserving selection . . . at the time. Seeing as how she's since disappeared off the face of the Earth, resurfacing briefly in 2002 to have a nervous breakdown during the taping of her *Unplugged* episode, fellow nominees the Dixie Chicks, or even PBS pledge drive/Christmas album behemoth Andrea Bocelli, were more deserving of the award.

2008: As of the writing of this book in 2011, '60s soul throwback/novelty singer Amy Winehouse hasn't released any music since she was named Best New Artist in 2008, but she has become a tabloid fixture for her remarkable ability to not die from the massive quantity and variety of drugs she openly consumes.

BEWILDERING NOMINATIONS

1960: One nominee was Edd "Kookie" Byrnes, the star of *77 Sunset Strip*, whose recording career consists almost entirely of the novelty song "Kookie, Kookie, Lend Me Your Comb." That year's winner, at least, was the respectable Bobby Darin.

1975: Marvin Hamlisch, a film composer, won. Though not really a performer per se, he did conduct and write "The Way We Were" for Barbra Streisand, and adapted century-old ragtime standards for *The Sting*. That's your National Academy of Recording Arts and Sciences, America: always on the cutting edge, getting behind this crazy ragtime the kids are into.

2001: Although Shelby Lynne was a 10-year, six-album veteran of country music, she won the Best New Artist award on the basis of her first mainstream rock album.

2004: Two new artist nominees in this year weren't new in the least. Fountains of Wayne was recognized for its *third* major-label album *Traffic and Weather* (they'd even had an alternative rock hit, "Radiation Vibe," seven years earlier) and Heather Headley, a well-known Tony Award–winning Broadway star with a long discography of cast recordings, was nominated behind her first *pop* album. (Evanescence won.)

Where do hobbits, unicorns, evil robots, powerful war-locks, and Satan come to life in stories that sound like they were written by lonely seventh graders?

Concept Albums

While the intent may be noble—to bring long-form sto-rytelling and/or mysticism to rock music—the end prod-uct is almost always silly and a middling success at best, because concept albums lack three-minute songs and a celebration of hedonism, which are what make rock music fun and popular.

CAMEL, *Music Inspired by* The Snow Goose (1975)

Paul Gallico's acclaimed 1941 novella *The Snow Goose: A Story of Dunkirk* is a sweet, sentimental story about a wounded goose that is nursed back to health by a little girl during World War II. The British prog rock band Camel wanted to make an album out of it, but Gallico wouldn't give them clearance. As related in the album's liner notes, for some reason Gallico thought Camel had something to do with Camel cigarettes, and he didn't want to promote smoking. That, coupled with a threat of copyright infringement if they went through with the album anyway, led the band to legally skirt Gallico's opposition by titling the album not *The Snow Goose*, but instead *Music Inspired by The Snow Goose*. In a further move to avoid direct comparisons to the novel and any subsequent litigation, the album was recorded without lyrics. It was a moderate success, reaching #22 on the British album chart.

ROGER WATERS, *Radio K.A.O.S.* (1987)

Bassist Roger Waters left Pink Floyd in 1985 when he realized he didn't need an entire band to create meandering and joyless concept albums. *Radio K.A.O.S.* tells the story of Billy, a boy in a vegetative state shut off from the world but in possession of an undiscovered gift—he can hear and transmit radio signals. (Waters might be hoping you confuse Billy with a deaf, dumb, and blind pinball wizard named Tommy.) Billy can also use radio waves to transmit his thoughts because his brother stashed a stolen cordless phone under the cushion of Billy's wheelchair. Billy then sends messages around the world, culminating in a faked launch of ballistic missiles to make humanity think that World War III is underway. Why? To show people the need for peace and common decency to prevent the real World War III from ever happening. Of course, since Billy can feel, think, empathize, interact, and strategize means he isn't really a vegetable after all. And speaking of plant life, few of the loyal and sizable Pink Floyd fan base bothered to put down the bong long enough to buy a copy of *Radio K.A.O.S.*, which topped out at #50 on the album chart and produced a couple of singles that performed marginally on rock radio.

STYX, *Kilroy Was Here* (1983)

Scene: In a bleak dystopian future, rock has been outlawed by fascists (fascists love zydeco, and only zydeco—

everybody knows that). Rock musician Robert Orin Charles Kilroy (R.O.C.K.) is thrown in jail for rocking until a group of rock-loving rockers help the rocker escape and stage a rock concert that rocks so hard it inspires humanity to overthrow the robots (with rock) and free the world from its captors' shiny metal claws, and to then rock freely. While this all seems like a really hard sell, *Kilroy Was Here* did include "Mr. Roboto," one of Styx's most familiar songs.

BLUE ÖYSTER CULT, *Imaginos* (1988)

Do you like old-fashioned arena rock, but not as much as comic books, and have you also joined a cult at some point in your life? Then you are the target audience for *Imaginos*. While it's commonly accepted that World War I began when a Serbian nationalist murdered the arch-duke of Austria, escalating the already mounting ethnic and political tensions across Europe, this is wrong. According to *Imaginos*, a group of mystical aliens called Les Invisibles started World War I with the help of a magical, thought-controlling mirror retrieved from a secret pyramid in Mexico by a shape-shifting, time-traveling psychic named Imaginos, who was born during the astrological alignment of Sirius and the Sun in 1804, leading him to become a servant of Les Invisibles. And they wanted him to keep the mirror in an attic in England, so he did, where it slowly drove the leaders of Europe insane, leading to the conflicts that culminated in World War I. This was all the idea of BÖC manager Sandy Pearlman, who conceived it in the late '60s, before the band even formed. Written throughout the '70s, recorded in 1982, and then shelved for six years, *Imagi-nos* peaked on the album chart at #122, the band's lowest showing since its 1973 debut.

QUEENSRŸCHE, *Operation: Mindcrime* (1988)

Evil scientist Dr. X brainwashes a drug addict named Nikki into killing his rivals. All Dr. X has to do is say the word "mindcrime" and Nikki switches into *Manchurian Candidate* mode. Despite being brainwashed, Nikki starts to feel guilty about all of the murdering and falls in love with a hooker-nun named Mary. Then Nikki and Mary bone on an altar, after which Mary kills herself and Nikki goes insane. *Mindcrime!* In 2009, *Playbill* reported that Broadway star Adam Pascal (he was in the original cast of the beloved HIV minstrel show *Rent*) wants to adapt this for the stage, and Queensrÿche lead singer Geoff Tate told MTV in 2006 that a film version was in the works, but all that had really happened was that he had personally hired a screenwriter to adapt it, and that he would then pitch it to movie studios himself. As *Mindcrime* has a very dark premise and limited appeal (it sold a million copies, but it took three years, and very few have sold since), it will probably never actually have to compete for entertainment dollars on Broadway with *Shrek: The Musical* or in cineplexes with *Shrek 5: Still Shrekin'. Mindcrime!*

CHRISTOPHER LEE, *Charlemagne: By the Sword and the Cross* (2010)

Lee, the extremely old and creepy actor who has appeared in Dracula movies, *Star Wars*, and the *Lord of the Rings* trilogy, choices which can only be attributed to some sort of lifelong quest to please a distant, nerdy father, is also quite possibly a demonic wizard or alien being and/or time traveler from the Dark Ages. So if anyone is going to record a concept album (the Dungeons & Dragons of recorded music), it's going to be the guy who played Saruman. And of course it's going to be a metal concept album. In 2010, at age 87, Lee collaborated with composer Marco Sabiu on *Charlemagne: By the Sword and the Cross*, the story of the first Christian emperor of Rome. Iconic wizard guy, metal, medieval themes, told via a metal band backed by a symphonic orchestra: all this would, in theory, make *By the Sword and the Cross* the most perfect concept album ever. It got some ironic, mocking attention on music blogs, but as symphonic metal is not such a big deal these days (nor has it ever been, nor will it ever be), it sold a microscopic number of copies. Because it was interesting not in execution, only in concept. (See what I did there? *Yeah.*)

One time this one lady heard Prince's dirtiest song, saw a few seconds of a goofy Van Halen video, and became convinced that America was broken, and that the only way to fix it was broad, non-contextualized censorship. Because

Tipper Gore, and Only Tipper Gore, Cares About Your Children

In 1984, senator's wife Tipper Gore bought Prince's *Purple Rain* for her 11-year-old daughter. They listened together, and when they got to "Darling Nikki," Tipper grew terrified. Somehow unaware that Prince is a sex-obsessed sex fiend who sings about sex almost all the time and in extremely graphic ways, the song's explicitness shocked her; the second line of the song talks about Nikki masturbating in the lobby of a hotel.

Wondering if such vulgarity was an isolated incident, Gore did some "research" by watching MTV. She tuned in long enough to find some more work that suitably appalled her, including Van Halen's "Hot for Teacher" and Mötley Crüe's "Looks That Kill," which Gore believed to be about, respectively, sex (actually about a crush, but the video features a girl in a bikini) and the latter about violence ("looks can kill" is an incredibly well-worn cliché; the song isn't really about physical attractiveness, or anything else, killing anyone).

Gore was bored enough to get herself worked up into a lather, then she called up her Washington political wife friends and found that they, too, were extremely bored and appalled once they found out for the first time that rock 'n' roll songs had lyrics about sex, violence, and drugs. In 1985, they formed the Parents Music Resource Center. Charter members: Gore, Susan Baker (wife of treasury secretary James Baker), Pam Howar (wife of a major Washington real estate broker), and Sally Nevius (wife of a Washington city councilman).

The PMRC sent a letter to 62 record companies, politely asking them to stop ruining America by turning its children into dildo-fellating crack whores by no longer releasing any material that they, the PMRC, found to be sexually explicit or violent. Of those 62 companies, just seven responded, and all of them, understandably, expressly declined to comply with Gore's audacious request.

They also rejected Gore's more reasonable offer: to enact an album rating system similar to the G/PG/R one used by the movies, so parents could tell at first glance what an album was all about. This was Gore's proposed ratings system: sexual content got an "X," violence got a "V," drugs and alcohol got a "D/A," and music with Satan worship or occult themes got an "O."

Since nobody in the music industry was willing to submit to overzealous arbitrary censorship, even when it was *for the sake of the children*, Gore and the PMRC used their clout (that is, Gore's husband, Senator Al Gore) to get the U.S. Senate to hold hearings in 1985 regarding the alarming content of popular music. The PMRC gave their piece about how the new phenomenon of sex, drugs, and violence in music was corrupting children, neglecting to remember or mention that their generation also grew up with rock music. Nor was it brought up that both Al and Tipper Gore were (and still are) major Grateful Dead fans, calling their credibility as judges of music into serious doubt.

Then some rock stars came in to the Senate chamber to testify against the PMRC. Who came, and what they said, was both surprising and amusing:

- **JOHN DENVER** stated he was "opposed to censorship of any kind" because he felt that censors have no artistic sensibility or sense of context. In 1973, he cites as an example, his song "Rocky Mountain High," earnestly and honestly about the glory of being outside amid the majesty of nature, was banned by many radio stations during an FCC crackdown on songs with drug references. Denver added that, "The suppression of the people of a society begins with the censorship of the written or spoken word. It was so in Nazi Germany." So yeah, the most conservative, square-looking dude in history thought that this was all a bad idea, and not just bad-bad, but *Hitler*-bad.

- **DEE SNIDER** of Twisted Sister, who began his testimony by identifying himself as a married, Christian, non-drinking father so as to point out the absurdity of trying to identify evil-hearted rock stars by outward appearances or recorded output, defended his band's song "Under the Blade," which was about his fear of an upcoming surgery. Tipper Gore had claimed it was about sadomasochism, bondage, and rape. "The only sadomasochism, bondage, and rape in this song is in the mind of Ms. Gore," Snider said to the panel, "and she found it." So Dee Snider turned the tables and basically called Tipper Gore a pervert.

- But the most pointed and thoughtful testimony came from **FRANK ZAPPA**. "The proposal is an ill-conceived piece of nonsense which fails to deliver any real benefits to children, infringes the civil liberties of people who are not children, and promises to keep the courts busy for years dealing with the interpretational and enforcemental problems inherent in the proposal's design," Zappa said.

The testimonials didn't do much to stop the crusade, though, and in November 1985, the Recording Industry Association of America, the music industry trade group, caved and created the "Parental Advisory: Explicit Lyrics" sticker to place on offending albums, short of the specific rating system Gore had wanted (nor was it legally binding).

But was it all an on-the-level, save-the-children situation? Maybe not. In his 1988 book *The Real Frank Zappa Book*, Zappa suggests that the PMRC hearings were a diversion. Two days before the stickering was announced, a Senate committee discussed the Home Audio Recording Act, a bill heavily supported by the RIAA. It would have put a tax on the sale of blank videotapes and audiotapes, which would then go to the RIAA, to reimburse them for what it claims was rampant piracy of people recording stuff off the radio and MTV. The act didn't pass, but one of its co-sponsors was, interestingly enough, Al Gore. Zappa theorized that the RIAA would agree to police itself (albeit in a watered-down, ineffectual way) if Sen. Gore helped push through a tax that would be lucrative for the music industry.

Fifteen years later, Al Gore ran for president. Who knows how many liberals, still with a sour taste in their mouth over a supposed fellow liberal like Gore helping his wife try to censor art, voted for Ralph Nader instead? Ultimately, Nader siphoned off Gore votes and George W. Bush won the election. So then, if you want to blame anybody for all the stuff that went wrong during Bush's term—the war in Iraq, the economic collapse—you can go ahead and just blame Tipper Gore for all of it.

During the Parents Music Resource Center hearings, the panel singled out 15 songs,

"The Filthy 15"

that they thought were particularly horrendous. Were these songs really that offensive, or did Tipper Gore and her repressed friends just have extraordinarily twisted imaginations?

PRINCE, "Darling Nikki"

Prince meets Nikki, a nymphomaniac masturbating with a magazine in a hotel lobby, though it's unclear if she's masturbating with a magazine or masturbating *with* a magazine. The song then details a wild, toy-powered night of debauchery. But at the end, when Nikki has left and Prince finds a letter in which Nikki thanks him for the sex and an open invitation to do it all again, this at least teaches kids the importance of writing thank-you notes.

SHEENA EASTON, "Sugar Walls"

This title supposedly is a reference to the walls of the vagina, which are, you know, metaphorically "sweet." If the vaginal walls are literally sweet, your lady friend has diabetes. Since that's a terrible thing to write a song about, the song is probably about waffle cones.

CYNDI LAUPER, "She Bop"

Lauper has only hinted that the song is about masturbation, although the lyrics and accompanying music video include many ironic references to going blind, a known result of onanism. But since she's never *outright* said it's about masturbation, "She Bop" could be about not the she bop, but a girl ("she") dancing ("bop"), or the teen idol magazine *Bop!* Hey, girls just want to have fun (by themselves).

VANITY, "Strap on Robbie Baby"

The title is merely British working-class slang meaning either "Fancy a pint of ale then?" or "Hey, put on this dildo." Probably the latter, because the writer of this song is Prince, a devoutly religious man who shuns alcohol but not dildos or sex fiends he meets in hotel lobbies.

TWISTED SISTER, "We're Not Gonna Take It"

A tongue-in-cheek song with cartoonish themes of rebellion (Twisted Sister does not like your rules, whatever they may be) by a cartoonish group of men in wigs and makeup that was apparently so deranged and corrupting that it couldn't possibly have been used in Midol commercials and as the theme song of the 2003 gubernatorial campaign of California Republican Arnold Schwarzenegger.

W.A.S.P., "Animal (Fuck Like a Beast)"

This song is not about fucking, exactly. It's about fucking like animals.

DEF LEPPARD, "High 'n' Dry (Saturday Night)"

Gore should have taken another band to task for its use of excessive alcohol references, as anyone familiar with the history of Def Leppard will never become a binge drinker, because binge drinking leads to drunk driving, which leads to car accidents, which is why the drummer from Def Leppard only has one arm.

MARY JANE GIRLS, "In My House"

The plot: The Mary Jane Girls are going to have sex with you. And their mentor Rick James will probably want to watch or chain you to an air conditioner for three days. The PMRC missed an opportunity for real music-related public service in that it should have just straight up banned Rick James. Not his songs—the actual person.

AC/DC, "Let Me Put My Love Into You" AND MADONNA, "Dress You Up"

"Let me put my love into you" and "dress you up in my love" sit at different levels of effective sexual euphemism. Evidently, the PMRC hated euphemisms almost as much as the blatant stuff and had grown so cynical (or repressed and lustful) that any mention of the word "love" to them meant "fucking."

JUDAS PRIEST, "Eat Me Alive"

Judas Priest lead singer Rob Halford kept the fact that he was gay hidden from his bandmates for years, even after enduring criticism for this song, which contains lyrics about eating someone alive and injecting steel rods at maximum velocity into body parts spread wide. Knowing there's a gay subtext makes the whole thing less misogynistic and harrowing and more, oh I don't know, what's the word, playful?

MÖTLEY CRÜE, "Bastard"

This song could be a valuable educational tool for the shiftless, directionless, juvenile heavy metal enthusiast. An attentive listen reveals a detailed, step-by-step account of how to viciously and effectively stab a man to death. It's good to learn a skill.

BLACK SABBATH, "Trashed"

Gore thought this song glorified and celebrated drunk driving. She clearly didn't get to the end of the song, where the narrator crashes his car and dies.

MERCYFUL FATE, "Into the Coven"

Even the most naive, square, out-of-touch parent wouldn't be fooled into thinking a song called "Into the Coven" was innocuous, unless they missed the "c" and figured it was a song about an Easy-Bake Oven.

VENOM, "Possessed"

This song is on the "Filthy 15" list because of occult and satanic themes. But a cursory glance at the lyric sheet's many mentions of unholy conceptions and Satan babies reveals that . . . yeah, okay, Tipper.

Before we all had white strings dangling out of our ears, everybody used to carry around ugly black pouches that held 10 scratched-up discs. Before that, the music came on tiny analog reels encased in plastic. And before that, people who enjoyed music didn't leave home, lest they need to hear their favorite LP or wax cylinder at a moment's notice. Here are some other audio delivery devices, the bad ones that never caught on, and for good reason. As they say,

Hate the Player

ULTRADISC. In the 1970s, hardcore audiophiles shamelessly spent thousands on high-end stereos, also called "hi-fi's" (but God forbid you ever call them that) or record players with speakers. But such exacting, self-professed golden-eared snobs quickly tired of playing the same old cheap copies of *Aja* or *Mettle* that everybody else had on the fancy equipment they loved more than their gold medallions and unfaithful trophy wives. Enter the Mobile Fidelity Sound Lab, which starting in 1977 made double-thick (and double-priced) LPs, loaded with intricately mastered, super-crisp recordings of popular albums.

In 1987, MFSL (not to be confused with MFSB, or KMFDM) introduced the logical successor to the thick LPs: Ultradiscs, compact discs coated in 24-karat gold. Reportedly, this made them sound better, although all the gold really did was make the CDs last longer because gold degrades slower than aluminum, the usual CD material. They did sound a *little* better than regular CDs (which themselves were a revolutionary novelty in sound mastery in 1987) because all Ultradisc releases were completely remastered recordings anyway. Playable on any old CD player (which, in 1987, cost about as much as a high-end hi-fi system did 10 years earlier), the first Ultradisc was a jazz sampler, quickly followed by stoner/nerd classics such as Queen's *A Night at the Opera*, Pink Floyd's *Dark Side of the Moon*, Supertramp's *Breakfast in America*, and lots and lots of Rush.

FAIL: Ultradisc, and the Mobile Fidelity Sound Lab, never really caught on. There just aren't enough audiophiles out there to buy albums they already own, especially when they are garishly and needlessly made of gold and cost $30 a pop.

MINIDISC. On paper, Sony actually had a pretty good idea with this one: The MiniDisc, launched in 1992, was a three-inch disc enclosed in a clear plastic case.

It had the sound quality of a CD, but was compact and durable like a cassette. Sony perpetuated a huge ad campaign—consisting mostly of a TV spot in which a happy MiniDisc user blasted Joe Satriani licks while chilling on the beach.

FAIL: The CD had just toppled the cassette as the dominant format, and consumers probably weren't too keen on the idea of replacing their entire music collections so soon after they'd already done so. Also, MiniDiscs cost about $20 (vs. $15 for a CD) and the average MiniDisc player was $500. Prerecorded MiniDiscs were discontinued, but blank ones are still widely used by musicians to record high-quality demo tapes that no one will ever, ever hear.

DATAPLAY. In 2002, a company called DataPlay unveiled a format also called DataPlay, which it touted to be the next big thing in music delivery. But things were already clearly going another way; at the time of DataPlay's launch, 250,000 iPods had already been sold, and sales were rapidly increasing. The DataPlay medium was a lot like the MiniDisc, only tiny . . . extremely tiny. Each DataPlay disc was 32 millimeters in diameter. That's about three centimeters, or a little more than an inch, which is just seriously comically small.

Also, despite pushing the aging concept of a physical format, the DataPlay organization tried to cash in on the downloading vogue by offering blank DataPlay discs. Each held 500 megabytes of music, less than the

700 megabytes you could fit on a blank CD-R. Plus, the iPods of 2002 held 20 gigabytes of music, the equivalent of 40 DataPlay discs, and you didn't have to switch them out, like CDs or tapes, which is the whole appeal of MP3 players.

FAIL: *Three centimeters!* You can actually still buy the discs, but only via special request, by emailing a Data-Play employee named "Dave" and seeing what he's got laying around. (Seriously. That's actually the protocol.) Dave will mail some to you . . . if he can find the damn things. I mean, they're *three centimeters* long, people.

Determining the worst songs of all time goes far beyond Vanilla Ice and William Hung; that stuff is just too obvious. Far more interesting, and worse, is a song that is transcendent in its horribility, created by a musical icon that should really have known better, even if it was conceived at a personal and professional low period. Brian Wilson's unreleased 1989 rap single "Smart Girls" is, quite possibly,

The Worst Song of All Time

By 1989, former Beach Boys mastermind Brian Wilson was a shell of his former self, beaten down by years of mental illness, drug addiction, and ill-advised treatment methods. But he did manage to record two albums in two years for Sire Records—1988's *Brian Wilson* and

1989's very uncomfortably titled *Sweet Insanity*. The former sold modestly and earned some good notices; the latter was outright rejected by Sire Records. To put into historical context of just how terrible Sire executives found *Sweet Insanity*, consider that this was just a few months after the rest of the Beach Boys had released "Kokomo."

The label may have been right. Generally, the first single off an album is the strongest track, a savvy marketing maneuver to drum up interest in an album before the public can know if it's any good or not. (Sort of like how all the funny parts of a movie are in its trailer.) If the logic holds, then *Sweet Insanity*, were it ever to be released, would be classified among the worst albums ever made, because its first single was its best song, and that first single was to be a track called "Smart Girls," which is the single worst piece of music ever put to tape.

There are so, so many awful, bewildering things in "Smart Girls." It opens with a big band–style saxophone riff, with '80s reverb and echo piled on high before cutting to a tinny, synthesized, pedestrian rap beat. Then it shifts to the startling, maniacal, haunting giggling of Dr. Eugene Landy, best known as the quack psychologist/con artist who micromanaged Wilson's life (with what he shrewdly claimed was "24 hour therapy") and took him for everything he was worth (his services cost $35,000 a month), even, supposedly, writing Wilson's autobiography, and coproducing and cowriting this here song. The laughing is not, exactly, Landy laughing at Wilson for his gullibility—Dr. Landy is the hype man, the Flava Flav to Wilson's Chuck D. Because this is a rap song.

The lyrics are delivered in the manner that a 47-year-old white man in 1989 who was only familiar with the form thanks to a Fruity Pebbles commercial would rap: with goofiness, a stilted flow just slightly out of step with the beat, and reflecting total cultural unawareness, similar to how your dad would attempt to rap in 1989 after seeing a rap song in a Fruity Pebbles commercial.

Wilson then herkily-jerkily introduces himself by name, and tells of his ability to magically write songs, just by waving his hand. Immediately after, a multi-tracked crowd tells us Wilson is "the original Beach Boy." The way they say it all in perfect, screamingly happy unison is exactly the same way this same crowd has let you know on so many occasions that you really ought to call the Ghostbusters, or that you are currently listening to "Cool 105!"

The meat of the song is a playful but clearly not earnest apology that nobody asked for or thought was necessary, in which Wilson laments celebrating in song mentally insignificant women, such as "Surfer Girl(s)," "California Girls" and Rhonda. Now, in his middle age, Wilson tells us, unconvincingly, that he's into smart girls: "Wouldn't it be nice if they gave PhDs / for strokin' me with hypotheses." Also: "Gimme a gal who teaches school / who's not afraid to break the rules." If his goal was to praise smart women, he failed, because the word "gal" is both painfully dated and condescending. Also, he seems to want to get a hand job from science.

The song was an ill-fated, ill-conceived, and not at all ill attempt at modernity and legitimacy—as if simply releasing a rap song (250 copies were pressed for fan club members and radio . . . which have been widely bootlegged since) because that's the new thing would make the kids buy your record. Rather than heralding the comeback of a true pop genius and demonstrating his ability to succeed in any form of music he tries, it's the musical equivalent of your dorky boss sporting a visible erection in his flat-front khakis hitting on your girlfriend at the company picnic to prove to himself that he's "still got it" after the divorce.

Only Wilson wouldn't ever hit on your girlfriend, because she's a smart girl, and he totally respects her for that.

<< ▭ >>

If Brian Wilson's "Smart Girls" is the worst song of all time, then Disney's 2005 project to revive and re-brand the innovative and influential—but never popular or widely understood—New Wave group Devo as a children's band is probably

The Worst Idea in Music History

Even worse than Chris Gaines.

DEVO never sold a lot of records ("Whip It" was their only top 40 hit), but they were always strikingly original in both music and presentation; how many other bands have extolled a philosophy, especially one as nihilistic as *de-evolution*, the idea that man is slowly de-evolving into mindless pudding? As a result, their songs were full of menace, irony, consumerist satire, self-loathing, and copious masturbation references. But for reasons still not quite understood, representatives from Walt Disney Records approached the members of Devo in 2005 and asked if they'd like to re-launch the Devo "brand" with a project called **DEVO 2.0**: a group of kids in flowerpot hats (technically, they're called "energy domes") singing sanitized versions of Devo's many non-hits.

Perhaps sensing the opportunity for some ultra-meta cultural sabotage from the inside, Devo excitedly signed on. On the debut album, *DEV2.0*, it's actually the original members of Devo playing the instruments; a group of handpicked 10- to 13-year-olds of both genders provide the vocals. Any and all potentially offensive lyrics, especially the ones about sex, violence, or the herd mentality, were awkwardly changed by Disney staff songwriters to ones of bland happiness and hollow self-affirmation:

- The groups that need to be eliminated in "Through Being Cool" were now cliques, not "ninnies and twits."
- The mention of a gun in "Big Mess," which meant penis in context, was changed to "fun."
- "Uncontrollable Urge" was no longer about sex and anxiety, but craving junk food.
- "Jerkin' Back 'N' Forth" was changed so that it was explicitly about dancing, not implicitly about masturbation.

It was unclear who the audience for *DEV2.0* was supposed to be: Would hardcore Devo fans buy this for their kids? Certainly not. Would kids buy this on their own? Never. The project quickly died; there have been no more Devo 2.0 releases.

CHAPTER 6

This Is the End

MTV is like a badass punk rocker who doesn't give a crap about the establishment, one who gets amused if he offends somebody's delicate sensibilities . . . if that badass punk rocker were a division of a giant media corporation micromanaged so as not to air anything that might upset in any way its advertisers or board of directors. This is why, on several occasions, many videos have been outright

Banned from MTV

This was, of course, a few years back; since then, MTV has banned all music videos.

GOLDEN EARRING, "When the Lady Smiles" (1984)

The Dutch band was just coming off the top 10 hit "Twilight Zone," the success of which was due in no small part to a popular video that featured, in what was rare at the time, a plot. (The plot involved spies; it didn't take much for a video to be impressive in 1983.) "When the Lady Smiles" would not become a hit song, partly because MTV banned the video. This one had a plot, too: Golden Earring's lead singer Barry Hay tries to rape a nun on a bus, and then a dog eats his brain. While we see this kind of thing all the time today on *Dancing with the Stars*, nun rape and brain-eating were just too risqué for mainstream consumption in 1984.

BILLY IDOL, "Hot in the City" (1987)

Idol first recorded "Hot in the City" in 1982 with a nondescript video, but re-released it in 1987 for a greatest hits compilation with a new video. It never aired on MTV because it showed Idol's girlfriend Perri Lister nailed to a cross, Jesus-style.

FOO FIGHTERS, "Low" (2003)

Foo Fighters videos are frequently funny, be it the Mentos commercial parody of "Big Me," or the fat suits/heroin/airplane high jinks of "Learn to Fly." "Low" might be the funniest one of all. In it, lead singer Dave Grohl and Jack Black play burly lumberjacks who meet up in a hotel room, get piss drunk, put on women's clothing, trash the room, and make sweet love. MTV didn't air it because of the homosexual content, which isn't actually depicted at any time on-screen, merely suggested.

MADONNA, "Justify My Love" (1990)

Though one of the most popular and powerful performers of the era, MTV decided not to air "Justify My

Love" because of voluminous and graphic sexual imagery (some of which involved a little person). In short, "Justify My Love" was reminiscent of an East German porno film and MTV freaked out. Madonna's career far from suffered. She released "Justify My Love" as a video single, and it sold more than a million copies, earning her far more money than the nothing she would have got had it just aired on MTV for a while.

MARILYN MANSON, "Coma White" (1999)

In early 1999, Manson filmed the video for "Coma White," the third single off of *Mechanical Animals*. Manson and his then-fiancée Rose McGowan play John F. and Jacqueline Kennedy in a reenactment of the president's 1963 assassination in Dallas. Tasteless? Of course, but in a press release, Manson claimed the video was about America's "unquenchable thirst for violence." Nevertheless, MTV upheld a ban on the video for most of 1999. Its premiere was indefinitely delayed out of sensitivity over the Columbine shootings in the spring, then again in the summer due to the death of John F. Kennedy Jr. MTV eventually aired the video in late 1999, by which point *Mechanical Animals* was no longer a top album that needed promotion.

THE LATE NIGHT HOURS

Many controversial videos were never banned outright. MTV is way too savvy to just not air the titillating videos, preferring to cause a public consciousness-boosting cultural fervor for a few weeks. For such videos, the network has employed a device called "late night rotation," in which the video is only to be played after 9:00 p.m.

- **CHER'S "IF I COULD TURN BACK TIME" (1989)**, because she prances around a naval battleship in a thong, fishnet body stocking, and leather jacket.
- **SIR MIX-A-LOT'S "BABY GOT BACK" (1992)**, due to the sheer volume of asses, ass-related imagery, and ass symbolism.
- **THE PRODIGY'S "SMACK MY BITCH UP" (1997)** aired well past midnight, and was introduced with a warning from MTV News anchor Kurt Loder, who looked like he could barely contain his contempt at having to tape such a disclaimer. After a week of complaints over the video's graphic sex scenes, female nudity, and a fight scene, MTV took it off the air for good, having aired it twice.
- **INCUBUS'S "MEGALOMANIAC" (2004)**, which on the broad angle is about corrupt leaders riding the cult of personality to fascistic heights of extreme power and the freedom from accountability. But as the song came out during the contentious 2004 election cycle, it's clearly about George W. Bush. The video, however, features images of Hitler, as well as people happily drinking oil (suggesting that the Bush-led Iraq War was about the United States trying to get control of Middle Eastern petroleum reserves). MTV banned the video because (1) Hitler is bad, and (2) it didn't want people to actually drink oil. MTV hates metaphors, but mostly lawsuits.

Say you're in a band. You are the lead singer, and you are odious. You are dictatorial, make poor musical choices, or have a drug problem that makes you unreliable. Or you die. Any number of these issues can make it difficult for the rest of the band to just fire you, but no matter:

You Can Be Replaced

First, the band "breaks up," and then once you're gone, they'll reunite under a different name, but with a similar sound and a new lead singer.

BAUHAUS – PETER MURPHY = LOVE AND ROCKETS

Bauhaus operated largely upon the whims of lead singer Peter Murphy, who left the goth band in 1983 for a somewhat successful solo career. He took the rights to the band's name with him, so the rest of the group (Daniel Ash, Kevin Haskins, and David J) continued as Love and Rockets, who were way more listenable and commercially successful than Peter Murphy ever was. Murphy's "Cuts You Up" was a minor hit, but Love and Rockets charted four albums and produced two modern rock staples, "No New Tale to Tell" and "So Alive," which reached #3 on the pop chart.

EVANESCENCE – AMY LEE = WE ARE THE FALLEN

With its listlessly played electric guitars and lyrical self-flagellation of modern youth fellowship masses, combined with the listlessly played electric guitars and lyrical self-flagellation of early '00s mook rock, the only tolerable thing about Evanescence was the powerfully voiced lead singer/corpse bride Amy Lee. Well, she was reportedly a bit of a controlling tyrant, and guitarist and cofounder Ben Moody left both the band and Lee, his childhood friend and sometime girlfriend, shortly after the band achieved commercial success in 2003. In 2007, Evanescence's Rocky Gray and John LeCompt also left the band and joined Moody to form We Are the Fallen. Not only is the name a sly dig at Evanescence (the band's 2003 debut was called *Fallen*), but they filled the Lee role with another pale, big-voiced brunette, Carly Smithson, a failed pop star in the late '90s Britney/Christina/Willa Ford vein and a sixth-place finisher on *American Idol* in 2008. We Are the Fallen's 2010 debut album *Tear the World Down* sold well, and the characteristically histrionic single "Bury Me Alive" got some airplay on rock radio, but it was nowhere near as successful as anything put out by Evanescence.

UNCLE TUPELO – JAY FARRAR = WILCO

Childhood friends Jay Farrar and Jeff Tweedy started Uncle Tupelo in 1987, the proponents of a new scene of music called alt country or No Depression, after the name of the band's first album and the magazine that covered these kinds of bands. Uncle Tupelo combined stark, rootsy, bare-bones country and folk music with the attitude and passion of modern alternative rock. But the longer the band stayed together, the longer Farrar and Tweedy blossomed as songwriters, each with their own extremely singular vision as to how Uncle Tupelo should proceed. After numerous onstage, backstage, and mid-recording scream-fests between the two, the group broke up in 1994 after four albums. Farrar immediately formed a new band in the Uncle Tupelo mold called Son Volt, which had the rock hit "Drown" in 1996. The rest of Uncle Tupelo, meanwhile, sided with Tweedy, and together they formed Wilco, one of the most influential, respected, and beloved rock bands of the '90s and 2000s. Their masterpiece *Yankee Hotel Foxtrot* went gold in 2002 and was named Album of the Year by *Rolling Stone*.

STONE TEMPLE PILOTS – SCOTT WEILAND = TALK SHOW

Scott Weiland is more famous at this point for taking heroin, not being able to stop taking heroin, and abusing his wife while on heroin than he is for "Plush," "Interstate Love Song," or "Big Bang Baby." In 1997, after three STP albums, Weiland grew estranged from the band due to his near-lethal drug habit as well as the desire to sporadically work on his solo album *12 Bar Blues* (although really, he was probably mostly just doing more heroin). So Dean DeLeo, Robert DeLeo, and Eric Kretz formed a "side project," Talk Show, which consisted of the entire group minus Weiland; Dave Coutts, an L.A. music veteran, was recruited to sing. Talk Show's only album *Talk Show* was released in 1997 and went nowhere. Weiland still had his problems, but STP reunited almost immediately.

JOY DIVISION – IAN CURTIS = NEW ORDER

The dreamy, atmospheric Joy Division formed in 1976 and were among the first groups signed to the legendary British label Factory Records. But when lead singer Ian Curtis, depressed over the breakup of his marriage (among many, many other things), hanged himself on May 18, 1980 (hours before the band was to leave for what surely would have been a star-making U.S. tour), the rest of the band opted to stay together, albeit with a new name. After adding in unofficial live keyboardist Gillian Gilbert to the group, Peter Hook, Stephen Morris, and Bernard Sumner (assuming lead vocals) debuted as New Order less than five months after Curtis's death.

Member #1 of popular, defunct band: Wow, we sure were an artistically and culturally significant band that sold millions of records and delighted hordes of people. *Member #2 of popular, defunct band:* We sure were. What say we get the band back together and give it another go? *Member #1 of popular, defunct band:* Yes, former bandmate,

Let's Get the Band Back Together! Wait, Let's Not. I Just Remembered That I Wish You Were Dead

THE SMITHS WERE LITIGIOUS

The most important bands of alternative rock are, as far as I'm concerned, Pixies, Nirvana, R.E.M., and the Smiths, who broke up in 1987. In 1991, Smiths drummer Mike Joyce sued Morrissey and guitarist Johnny Marr for $1 million of royalties he claimed were never paid. Joyce won the suit; Morrissey was so miffed that he told reporters that the Smiths wouldn't and couldn't play together ever again. In 2005, organizers of the Coachella Festival offered the Smiths $5 million to play just one set. Morrissey's response, as he told *Uncut* magazine: "I'd rather eat my own testicles than reform the Smiths, and that's saying something for a vegetarian."

TALKING HEADS HATE DAVID BYRNE

By the end of the '80s, the members of Talking Heads who weren't front man David Byrne had become a reluctant tool for the musical whims of David Byrne. For example, the 1986 album *True Stories* was comprised of songs from Byrne's big screen musical comedy *True Stories*, and the 1988 album *Naked* was all about African music, because that's what Byrne was into at that moment. The band officially broke up in 1991, and Byrne continued on with his solo career. (He'd already released two albums while still with Talking Heads that were far too esoteric to even put his bandmates through—one was some pretentious world music jerkoffery; the other was a classical piece.)

In 1996, the rest of the group swallowed their pride and approached Byrne to make a new Talking Heads album. He didn't want to, so they formed a "new" band called the Heads and released an album called *No Talking, Just Head*. The group in its entirety played at its 2002 Rock and Roll Hall of Fame induction, but probably will never play together again, as drummer Tina Weymouth later called Byrne—curiously, to several reporters, in exactly the same way—"incapable of returning friendship." Byrne, however, told Australian newspaper the *Age* that a reunion was unlikely because he and the others were "musically miles apart." One of those highly advanced Byrne projects that's so beyond the rest of Talking Heads, by the way, was a 2005 stunt in which he converted an abandoned paint factory in Sweden into a gigantic, working organ.

THE BEATLES WERE TOO TIRED

In the first few years after they split in 1970, the Beatles were routinely offered huge sums of money to reunite, but tensions were so high (and solo careers so lucrative) that it never happened. So in April 1976 on *Saturday Night Live*, executive producer Lorne Michaels appeared in a sketch to make a direct appeal to the band: If they appeared on the show, he'd give them the comically low sum of $3,000 to be shared any way they saw fit. ("If you want to give less to Ringo, that's up to you," Michaels half joked.) The sketch was well received—but no response from the Beatles came in. So, a couple of weeks later, Michaels upped the offer . . . by $200.

In a bizarre coincidence that's become Beatle lore (corroborated afterward by both Paul McCartney and

John Lennon), McCartney and Lennon were actually hanging out together that night. At Lennon's apartment. In New York City. About six blocks from the NBC studios where they were broadcasting *Saturday Night Live*. And they were watching *Saturday Night Live* on TV at the moment Michaels offered them $3,200 to make an appearance. All things considered, they talked about going down to NBC to actually take up Michaels on the joke offer, but ultimately decided that it was too late, and that they were too tired.

No Beatles reunion ever happened—Lennon died in 1980, and George Harrison died in 2001. The only remaining possibility for a Beatles reunion is if Ringo and Paul get together, which they often do, for coffee, because Ringo works at the Starbucks in Paul's neighborhood.

ABBA WAS HONEST

While its songs formed the basis of the Broadway musical *Mamma Mia!* and its movie adaptation, the four members of ABBA have made very few public appearances since they stopped performing and recording together in 1982. That's by design—they don't want to reunite. In 2000, a promoter offered the group $1 billion for a 100-date concert tour. They declined—they declined a *billion* dollars. Member Björn Ulvaeus has said on numerous occasions that ABBA will never play together again because what they would sound like now would pale in comparison to how they did in their heyday.

Even if you've sold millions of records, you're still going to die, most likely in a freaky, horrendous way. Because

Rock Stars Do the Deadliest Things

JIMI HENDRIX didn't die of a drug overdose. Technically, he took too many sleeping pills on the night of September 17, 1970, and was too zonked out when his body tried to repel the drugs. He vomited, inhaled the vomit, asphyxiated on the vomit, and died.

JOHN BONHAM of Led Zeppelin was a huge drinker, but he didn't die of alcohol poisoning, although booze very directly contributed to his death at age 32. En route to a rehearsal on the morning of September 24, 1980, Bonham stopped for breakfast, which was 16 shots of vodka. He continued to drink throughout the day, and on the afternoon of September 25, he was found dead. Like Hendrix, Bonham had inhaled and choked on his own vomit. A coroner determined that in the 24 hours before he died, Bonham had knocked back 40 vodka shots.

Toto drummer **JEFF PORCARO** died of a heart attack in 1992 at age 38. Generally, only one thing causes the death at age 38 of a guy who makes rock music for a living: cocaine. Some news outlets dutifully reported that

that was what had killed Porcaro, but the coroner's report was wildly misinterpreted. A trace amount of cocaine had been found in the drummer's body, which could have been in there for a decade or more. What *really* killed Porcaro was yard work. He had an allergic reaction to a pesticide, his body went into panic mode, that triggered a heart attack, and then he died.

Who drummer **KEITH MOON**'s death is terribly ironic. Well known for drinking booze by the gallon, Moon actually died in 1978 of an overdose of a prescription medication that doctors gave him to control and eventually kick his alcohol cravings.

Ever hear that tasteless joke, "If **KAREN CARPENTER** and **MAMA CASS** had shared that ham sandwich, they'd both be okay"? Yeah, it's not funny. Carpenter was anorexic and Cass Elliot (The Mamas and the Papas) was very overweight. But the joke isn't just unfunny, it's also inaccurate: Karen Carpenter didn't die of anorexia—she died of a heart attack. At the time of her death in 1983, she was receiving treatment for anorexia. No longer starving herself to death, the treatment, ironically, killed her. She'd gained so much so rapidly—to get to a healthy weight—that it caused too much stress on her heart, already compromised from years of anorexia, and it gave out.

Elliot also died of a heart attack, not from, as has been widely disseminated over the years, choking on a ham sandwich. A ham sandwich was found near her body (in the same apartment where Keith Moon would die four years later) and the detail was simply listed in the coroner's report. That detail was leaked to the press, which instantly and permanently created the urban legend/fat joke that the heavyset Cass died while eating.

DENNIS WILSON of the Beach Boys, while drunk on his boat in 1983, decided to go fetch some mementos of his ex-wife that he'd thrown into the ocean . . . in a fit of passion years earlier. He didn't have much success—he drowned almost immediately.

JEFF BUCKLEY went swimming in a Mississippi River tributary one dark night in 1997 with all of his clothes and his boots on. He drowned.

Afrobeat innovator and world music icon **FELA KUTI** believed that AIDS was a myth. Perhaps Fela changed his mind in 1997, shortly before he died from the AIDS-related illnesses he had, which his body couldn't fight off because he had AIDS.

While completely sober at a party in 1978, Chicago's original lead guitarist **TERRY KATH** grabbed a .38, put it up against his temple, and told friends, "Don't worry, it's not loaded." He was half right, for while there were no bullets in the magazine, there was one in the chamber. Kath pulled the trigger, instantly accidentally killing himself. Baby, what a big surprise.

Musicians: Here are a few simple guidelines to follow when writing, recording, and releasing music so as not to ruin all the fame and fortune you've accumulated or wish to accumulate. Yes, yes, rock 'n' roll is supposed to be about rebellion, but it's not 1955 or 1977 anymore. So just do what I say and follow

The Rules

and you'll be fine.

DO NOT IMBUE YOUR LYRICS WITH POP CULTURAL REFERENCES. In six months, they will sound dated; in two years they will sound ironically hilarious; and after that, they will sound dated once more.

House of Pain's "Jump Around" should be a perfectly serviceable early '90s song to sing along to in your car during your local radio station's "Retro Café Flashback" or whatever, but it is not. This is because of a line that mentions playing Sega. Good one, House of Pain—way to reference what turned out to be an also-ran in the video game wars of two decades ago. Did nothing rhyme with "TurboGrafx-16"?

Another example is Prince's "Kiss," in which he informs a lady that a good personality doesn't come from following the crowd . . . specifically, watching the popular '80s nighttime soap *Dynasty*. If it's 2011 and you're still watching *Dynasty*, having enough attitude is a minor problem, ranking far below the fact that you're a morbidly obese shut-in who watches *Dynasty* reruns on a low-wattage UHF station from Mexico.

SOLUTION: Avoid cheap pop cultural references that are vaguely familiar enough to pull in listeners. Go for songs about the human condition—you want your songs to be timeless, non–era specific, perennial classics . . . that generate perennial royalty checks.

IF YOU RELEASE THE ONE SONG THAT IS THE MOST UNREPRESENTATIVE OF YOUR SOUND AS A SINGLE AND IT BECOMES A BIG HIT, YOU CANNOT DISOWN THE SONG. You can't trash it, you can't tell the media you hate it to seem disaffected, and you can't skip it at a concert. While we understand that you want to grow as a musician, you can't pretend that you didn't, at one point, make a quick cash grab by releasing the most commercial song you had as a single. If you recorded it and millions of people bought it, that means millions of people loved it, and if you don't play it in concert, they'll resent you for it and think you're unappreciative of your fans and also pretentious.

Nirvana didn't play "Smells Like Teen Spirit" after 1992, Radiohead doesn't play "Creep" at concerts anymore, R.E.M. hasn't played "Shiny Happy People" in 20 years, and Nada Surf very, very rarely plays its *only* actual hit, "Popular." While I am a fan of the catalogs of all those bands, I would really want to hear in person the songs I grew up on, dammit. (One exception: Ben Folds doesn't have to play "Brick" live ever again if he doesn't want to, because that song is about Folds taking his girlfriend to get an abortion the day after Christmas—he shouldn't have to revisit that moment every night.)

SOLUTION: Take a lesson from KISS, who continued to include its biggest hit in its live act, the strings-heavy ballad "Beth," even after its singer and writer Peter Criss left the band. They just made his replacement Eric Carr sing it.

So just play the song, you sellout. We *like* the song.

IF YOU WRITE A LOVE SONG THAT'S SPECIFICALLY ABOUT YOUR SPOUSE OR LOVER, DON'T TELL THE WORLD THAT THE SONG IS ABOUT THAT SPOUSE OR LOVER. This will cause the relationship to end, and you'll still have to perform the song at every concert you play from now until forever.

While the honest sentiment will make it one of your most beloved, unforgettable, and popular songs, a personal love song is ultimately like tattooing a mate's name on your arm: It will curse you into breaking up. So there you'll be, performing a love song forever and ever about a person you loathe, who maybe cheated on you, or who took all of your money, or who won't let you see your kids, or who is threatening to put a sex tape of you up on the Internet.

Billy Joel wrote the lovely "Just the Way You Are" about his first wife, Elizabeth Weber. The song went to #3 in 1978, sold half a million copies, and then Joel won the Grammys for both Record of the Year and Song of the Year. Joel and Weber divorced in 1982. *Cursed*. But

Weber remained part of her ex-husband's management team, which also included Weber's brother, who embezzled millions from Joel. *Cursed*. But Joel lived to love again, marrying supermodel Christie Brinkley in 1985. Unwisely ignoring the curse, he wrote many songs for Brinkley, most notably the 1993 hit "All About Soul," because, clearly, there is no one more soulful than a dead-eyed supermodel. In 1994, Joel and Brinkley divorced. *Cursed*.

SOLUTION: If you write a love song about a specific person, this is a very special, very private thing—so make it a special, private gift for that person.

FINALLY, DON'T USE THE FRONT MAN'S LAST NAME AS THE NAME FOR YOUR BAND. This rule does not refer to Bruce Springsteen and the E Street Band, or Ben Folds Five, or the Dave Matthews Band. It means to not just use a last name as the band name. In the history of recorded music, it's only really popped twice: Dio and Van Halen. For Dio, it worked because *dio* is Italian for "God," and Ronnie James Dio was the god of metal. It clicked for Van Halen because it's a Nordic name and is thus de facto way metal. Other guys name bands after themselves for reasons of ignorance and false hope: that a single surname implies a band that shall rock majestically from on high. In other words, these guys think that they sound like Dio or Van Halen. They do not. The name will just remind listeners of Dokken, Winger, Nelson, Bon Jovi, Daughtry, and Hanson.

SOLUTION: Have some fun; make up a name. How often in life have you heard a non sequitur, and you or somebody around you mentioned that it would make a great band name? This is why there are bands with names like Southern Culture on the Skids, Smashing Pumpkins, Green Apple Quick Step, Moby Grape, and Ween. These people are musicians, and they put in the effort of trying to express themselves, and their band's music, through a name. Sure, they can certainly be outwardly ridiculous, but they're fun, and you know what you're getting.

And what you're not getting is Winger.

≪ACKNOWLEDGMENTS≫

The process of writing my first book was as exciting and novel as I thought it would be, but it was also really smooth. Credit for that goes to a marvelous editor, Maria Gagliano Scalora at Perigee Books. I was quite fortunate to land an editor who truly got what I was trying to do and who made sure that it was executed perfectly. An extended thanks to the editorial board, design team, and publicity department at Perigee, too.

But there wouldn't be a book without Dawn Frederick of the Red Sofa Literary Agency, who has provided endless amounts of wisdom, patience, and advice. She shot for the moon and got there.

My appreciation to those who read portions of the book early on and advised me on how to make it better: Doug, Marie, John, Jill, Jada, Ellie, Kasia, and Eric. Another round of thanks to everyone online who has helped promote this book and its blog with links and endorsements, particularly Jeremy Barker at the *Sunbreak* and Garry Vander Voort at Retroist.com.

My wife was the one who said that I should start writing about music. That was a good idea.

<<ABOUT THE AUTHOR>>

BRIAN BOONE has accomplished a lot, now that he has to write it all down. Most notably, he wrote this book.

For the better part of a decade, he's been a writer and editor for the bestselling Uncle John's Bathroom Reader series of trivia and nonfiction titles.

Brian has written for the theater, both musical and legitimate, writing the book and composing the music for *The Sea Is a Restless Whore*, a musical about pirates, which enjoyed a modest run on the West Coast. His absurdist comedy *The Egg Play* has been performed at community and school programs around the country.

He blogs with much wit about music and pop culture, as he does in this book, at LoveHateSociety.com, and with much wit about other topics at BrianAdamsBoone.com. He contributes to several other entertainment and information sites.

None of this served him particularly well when he was a contestant on *Jeopardy!* in 2009. He dominated the board, then blew all his money on the Daily Doubles, and came in third. But at least he got all the music questions correct.

He lives in southern Oregon with his family.